Entertaining Angels

by

Stephen Deal

John Duckworth

Bridget Foreman

Steve Newman

Les Padfield

Nick Page

Adrian Plass

With music by Michael Card

BIBLE SOCIETY

BRITISH AND FOREIGN BIBLE SOCIETY

Stonehill Green, Westlea, Swindon, SN5 7DG, England

A catalogue record for this book is available from the British Library ISBN 0564 041165

Printed in Great Britain by Swindon Press

Cover illustration by Chris Wigmore

Design and typesetting by British and Foreign Bible Society Graphic Services

Bible Societies exist to provide resources for Bible distribution and use. The British and Foreign Bible Society (BFBS) is a member of the United Bible Societies, an international partnership working in over 180 countries. Their common aim is to reach all people with the Bible, or some part of it, in a language they can understand and at price they can afford. Parts of the Bible have now been translated into over 2,000 languages. Bible Societies aim to help every church at every point where it uses the Bible. You are invited to share in this work by your prayers and gifts. The Bible Society in your country will be very happy to provide details of its activity.

Contents

Acknowledgements

Special thanks are due to the following:

Michael Card for generous permission to use songs from his repertoire as a central part of the *Entertaining Angels* revue, Barbara Emerson at Michael Card Music in the USA for her helpfulness, CopyCare Ltd in the UK for permission to reproduce Michael's music and lyrics; Brian Lincoln and Robin Noad for the *Entertaining Angels* concept and the authors who turned the idea into reality.

Introduction

by Nick Page and Lindsay Shaw

ONE: Right . . .

TWO: Here we are then.

ONE: Absolutely.

TWO: Are you ready?

ONE: Ready when you are. Totally prepared. As prepared as a boy scout who is specially prepared for "being very prepared week".

TWO: You have no idea what we're doing, have you?

ONE: Er . . . no.

TWO: We're the introduction.

ONE: Introduction to what?

TWO: *Entertaining Angels*.

ONE: I see. Juggle, do they?

TWO: Who?

ONE: These angels. Are they jugglers?

TWO: No.

ONE: Oh. Acrobats?

TWO: No.

ONE: Tap dancers? Plate spinners? Balinese hamster impressionists?

TWO: No.

ONE: Well, they're not very entertaining so far.

TWO: It's not that kind of entertainment. It's a collection of thespian delights that pinpoint for a postmodern world the relevance of the divine word.

ONE: Do what?

TWO: It's a load of sketches about the Bible.

ONE: Well why didn't you say so? Are they funny?

TWO: Very.

ONE: Challenging?

TWO: Absolutely.

ONE: Even moving.

TWO: Occasionally. I mean, they're all about how the Bible really tackles the things that matter – the things everyone thinks about. Hope . . .

ONE: Forgiveness . . .

TWO: Identity . . .

ONE: Food.

TWO: Food?

ONE: Well I think about it a lot.

TWO: As it happens, you can have food with these sketches too!

ONE: Really?

TWO: Yes, put ten or so together and stage a whole evening's revue.

ONE: With music?

TWO: Exactly. There are sixteen sketches – ideal for any meeting or outreach. Best of all, you can select ten of them, add in the songs provided and put on your own, full-length revue.

ONE: I like the sound of it so far.

TWO: You wait, it gets better. All of the sketches will get people thinking about the importance of the Bible as the guide and inspiration for everyday living. Four of them have been specially written to look at how the Bible addresses life issues highlighted by the Open Book project. The ones looked at here concern people's search for identity, hope, and forgiveness.

ONE: You mean "It's an ideal resource for churches looking to perform drama and music as part of their teaching in church as well as in sensitive evangelism with their neighbours."

TWO: I couldn't have put it better myself.

ONE: Thank you.

TWO: A lot of this material has been road-tested as well. It began life as the script for a special cabaret-style revue that was taken up and performed by a number of churches around the country.

ONE: And I can't help noticing that it comes with loads of help on how to do the sketches, with detailed notes on performance and loads of material to help you.

TWO: I think you're getting the hang of this introduction business.

ONE: Hang on, I feel some bullet points coming on . . .

The book contains:

- Guidance on presenting *Entertaining Angels*. This gives fuller details of how you might stage a full revue-style event.

- Sheet music and lyrics for six songs by singer-songwriter Michael Card.

- Notes on performance written by Les Padfield who directed the first revue performance of most of the material. These are offered as guidance and ideas that can be used as little or as much as you find helpful.

- Performance notes by the authors of the Open Book sketches. These appear before the sketches themselves.

- Three "link" sketches that were written to (1) introduce the revue, (2) introduce the second half, (3) introduce the concluding sketch, *The Five-Minute Bible*.

- A sample programme.
- Artwork that you can enlarge and use in creating your own publicity.

TWO: Have you quite finished?

ONE: Sorry, I got carried away there.

TWO: Now, a few words about the cast . . .

ONE: Tell them about the cast.

TWO: I'm doing it!

ONE: Sorry.

TWO: Now, you won't need . . .

ONE: Tell them how they won't need a cast of thousands for this. A minimum of six actors will do, plus a sound and a lighting engineer, and either a competent pianist/keyboard player and a good, confident singer . . .

TWO: Will you stop interrupting!

ONE: Or they could simply use recordings of the songs.

TWO: Shut up!

ONE: Oh, and don't forget to tell them that they could always opt for the grand scale and recruit up to thirty actors depending on whether people act in one or more sketches (and how many lines people want to learn) and a full music band.

TWO: **WILL YOU BE QUIET!!!!!!!**

ONE: [*Shocked*] There's no need to use bold uppercase.

TWO: I'm sorry.

ONE: [*Hurt*] I was only encouraging them to think big.

TWO: Quite.

ONE: [*Deeply upset*] I mean, if you'd done your introducing properly I wouldn't have had to make so many points.

TWO: Look, I've said I'm sorry. And stop putting all your emotions in brackets.

ONE: [*Insincerely*] I won't do it again.

TWO: Oh, I give up. Come on, let's get out of here.

ONE: Don't you think we ought to say more? Maybe about getting together with other churches to do a joint venture or something.

TWO: No, let's leave it now.

ONE: But I want to know what happens! Will they take the challenge? Will they use these sketches to open the Book to their community?

TWO: Well, let's go and sit at the bottom of the page or something, and see if they read any further.

ONE: OK. Last one on the page number's a cherubim!

How to stage Entertaining Angels
by Robin Noad and Lindsay Shaw

Conversation was animated as the arts centre emptied. All down the line now snaking from the theatre, people were eagerly swapping impressions. Some expressed how much they had enjoyed the evening's originality and humour, while others said how up to date the Bible had become and how long-known truths had jumped up suddenly and walloped them between the eyes . . .

The goal

The Bible is so much more than a book on paper. As the living word of God, it is capable of speaking to people through a whole variety of media – from drama and music to storytelling and song. Evenings of biblical drama, like that described above, or single sketches performed to illustrate a talk or discussion, can communicate sharply how up to date and relevant the Bible is to people's modern situations.

It is for this reason that *Entertaining Angels* was commissioned. Recent Bible Society research has found that one in three regular churchgoers will not have read the Bible in the last year. The *Entertaining Angels* revue and the individual sketches it offers are part of Bible Society's Open Book campaign to show that the Bible is alive, relevant and credible in a society and culture that, if it knows the Bible at all, dismisses it as outdated fable.

Through a variety of creative activities, the Open Book aims to help the Church demonstrate the Bible's relevance to key questions for individuals and society, like identity, freedom, justice, hope and forgiveness. Several sketches towards the back of this book will help you spotlight three of these.

We have been keen to make *Entertaining Angels* as versatile and flexible as possible. Whether you want to sprinkle one or two sketches through your regular (or special) meetings, or be more ambitious and stage a full evening revue as a number of churches have, you will find what you need here.

Using individual sketches

This is as simple as it sounds. Any sketches from this book can be inserted into a meeting as appropriate, whether you use single sketches or several that work well together.

We have also provided a separate section of Open Book sketches that appears at the end of this book. Because, in general, these will work better in situations where the specific themes can be explained and expanded upon, we have not included them in the *Entertaining Angels* revue. Another reason for separating them has been that some are written in a more realistic, though still humorous style. A keynote of this book is variety!

The revue: who do you need?

Let's assume, though, that you want to tackle an *Entertaining Angels* revue. What size of cast and support team do you need?

Firstly, it's important to say that an *Entertaining Angels* revue can be as simple or as imaginative as you want. You know your churches' capabilities, experience and situation better than we do. (Though some enquiries among your congregation and church leaders, if you are not one yourself, may unearth a surprising pool of talent and experience.)

Nor, as mentioned before, do you have to take the whole event on the shoulders of your own church. *Entertaining Angels* is an ideal opportunity to get to know the Christians "down the road" better, and for churches to work together.

In short, the number of performers you need is very flexible: a minimum of six and as many as thirty – depending on whether people act in one or more sketches (and how many lines they want to learn), and whether the performers are multi-talented and can sing, play and act! Most of the parts can be played by either women or men with the minimum of rewriting.

We would, however, encourage as many people to be involved as possible. If this can encompass other fellowships as well, so much the better. As well as fostering co-operation, it will also help from the practical view of selling tickets – if a cast of thirty sells just two tickets each, you already have an audience of sixty, not to mention all the other people who will be helping "behind the scenes".

The revue: how long is the performance?

A full revue using all eleven of the sketches in the *Entertaining Angels* revue section of this book would last about ninety minutes. However you could, if you wished, select a shorter programme and omit some sketches and songs. Again, it's up to you.

The revue: how and where can it be staged?

Our original idea (which we tried out very successfully in the first production) was to perform the revue "cabaret" style – with people seated around tables. A meal was served during the interval and a multiple-choice general knowledge (not Bible knowledge!) quiz given out before the performance began acted as an "ice-breaker". The quiz answers were given out as part of the link that led into the second half (page 41; see also "Notes on Performance"). With the interaction of eating and completing the quiz together, we felt this approach would help strangers to feel relaxed together and encourage discussion about what the audience had seen and heard. The meal itself could range from a simple "ploughman's supper" to a full-blown three-course meal. Alternatively, you might decide to serve refreshments only – whatever seems most appropriate given your local context and community.

Scenery

Scenery, props and make-up can all be kept very simple, but in order to create the right atmosphere we would strongly recommend the use of some simple stage lighting. The first performance included use of a video projector – but this is optional.

Music

The music is an integral part of the evening – often providing the positive, more serious view to contrast with the humour of the sketches. From various angles, the songs show the importance of listening to God's voice through the Bible, the challenge of the life of faith and the reality of being accompanied on that journey by Jesus the living Word. A recommended programme order, including songs and sketches, is shown on page 22.

All of the songs we have chosen come from the singer/songwriter Michael Card. As well as a gifted songwriter and musician, Michael is also a biblical scholar and has published Bible studies on the life of Christ and a commentary on St John's Gospel. His love of the Bible is reflected in nearly all his lyrics and makes his songs especially appropriate for the revue.

While we have obtained permission to include the sheet music for these songs in the publication, please note that you will probably need to obtain a performance licence from the Performing Rights Society when using them in the revue, and in any situation apart from a worship service. If you do not have a copying licence from Christian Copyright Licensing with the extension to copy music, you will need to obtain this (or contact CopyCare Ltd, the music copyright holders) before making any extra music copies. Further details are given on page 88.

Although you do not need to limit yourself to our selection of songs, we would encourage you to choose (or write?) material that also clearly highlights the relevance, challenge and joy of living in the light of the Bible. To make a balanced presentation, we recommend performing six musical items during the revue. You could of course add more music before or after the performance, or during the interval.

It is especially important to have a competent pianist/keyboard player and a good, confident singer. Of course, the band could be much larger than this minimum, with guitars, percussion and a melody instrument (such as clarinet or flute) being the ideal. Again this needs to reflect the resources and gifts of those involved.

As an alternative, it would be possible simply to play the appropriate tracks from a CD and project suitable slide images on to a screen or interpret these in dance or mime. In whatever way you use recorded music, it is important to have some visual or live performance to complement the music.

Please note that if you are going to use recorded music you will need to get a performance licence from Phonographic Performance Limited (details on page 89).

The venue

As far as venue goes you could use anything from a local church to a local theatre. Bear in mind, however, how easy it will be for the audience to see and hear, and choose a venue with which you and your audience will feel comfortable. Cost is, of course, another important factor.

As a rough guideline we would suggest you look for an audience of around 150–200 people for each performance. You can perform *Entertaining Angels* as a one-off event, or run it for several nights either at the same venue or possibly do a short local "tour".

The revue: how much will it cost to perform?

Depending on how much you are able to borrow, beg and get donated from friendly contacts you should be able to produce *Entertaining Angels* for as little as £300–£500 (for lighting, sound, etc., but not including food and assuming a free-of-charge venue). These costs could easily be covered from the sale of tickets though you will obviously need someone to act as event treasurer to draw up a budget and manage the costs. We have included a list of committee roles – to help you think through this and other "behind the scenes" roles that are so essential to having a successful event.

Achieving your goal

Of course, producing a high quality event such as this will involve a lot of hard work for the many people who will be involved, whether performing or carrying out tasks behind the scenes. However, our first production proved it can also be a hugely worthwhile and enjoyable experience, and have some long-term benefits for the individuals and groups involved.

There will be many ways in which you will be able to gauge the revue's success. If it succeeds as a spur to future creative activities, makes a splash within your community, and if it prompts performers and audience to think again about the place the Bible has in their lives, it will have been more than worth all the creative and practical energy you poured into it.

Getting from Here to There: Finding your Team

by Robin Noad

An essential first step before embarking on an event of this kind is to secure the backing and support of your church leaders. As well as helping you to promote the idea of the revue to your own congregation, it will probably be appropriate for them to make first contact with other local fellowships too who might also be involved.

Once you have the "green light" from your church leader, you will need to draw together a team of people with specific jobs to do. Some of the roles or tasks given below could be combined. Obviously all the members should be competent, enthusiastic, and be able to spare the necessary time. It is advisable that they are also representative of a range of churches to involve the widest variety of local fellowships.

Chairperson

This role should be a supervisory one, allocating the jobs and monitoring how well they are carried out.

- Allocate roles.
- Confirm that the job descriptions of all members will satisfactorily cover the work required.
- Agree targets and timetables for tasks.
- Convene meetings to blend individual members into a team; to monitor progress and to make decisions on issues arising.
- Arrange for notes of meetings to be kept.
- Identify when any members need extra help.

Director

Responsible for the dramatic presentation.

- Publicise and hold auditions.
- Assign parts, schedule, plan and direct rehearsals.

Stage Manager

Responsible for physical and technical facilities needed to stage the production.

- Check stage size needed, and its position. Arrange for stage blocks to be borrowed if necessary.
- Appoint sound and lighting technicians. Ensure liaison between them and the director.
- Arrange loan or hire of lights and public address system (PA) as appropriate.
- Where hiring is involved, ensure that this is accomplished within the budget agreed by the treasurer.

- On the day, support the director in every possible way to maximise the effect of the production.
- Keep an eye on the safety aspects of the equipment.

Musical Director

Work with and under supervision of the director to provide musical content for the production.

- Gather musicians.
- Arrange and lead musical rehearsals and ensure high standard of musical performance.

House Manager

Overall responsibility for the venue (except for the stage area), and for the audience.

- Check the availability of seating/tables. Borrow where necessary.
- Liaise with box office ticketing officer to ensure that the right number of tickets are issued.
- Appoint chief steward to sign up a team of volunteers as stewards to welcome and direct the audience. (There is an important safety element here so all the stewards should be mature people.)
- Arrange for stewards to arrive well before the performance to set the seating and tables as appropriate, and stay to ensure that the venue is left as you found it.

Publicity Officer

Ensure that the publicity materials are well and effectively distributed.

- Agree publicity strategy – including the quantity of leaflets/posters needed to cover requirements by churches, any appropriate mailings, and other local sites (shops, libraries, and so on.)
- Liaise with chairperson about possible local mailings which may be available.
- Agree print budget for posters and handbills with treasurer and arrange printing.
- Liaise with box office ticketing officer and arrange printing of tickets.
- Ensure distribution of publicity. Organise a team of volunteers?
- Co-ordinate with church liaison officer to encourage local fellowships to make best use of the materials; and keep churches well stocked.

General Promotion Officer

Ensure wide coverage of the event through local media. This is partly to help sell the tickets but, more importantly, to establish in the minds of the general public – who will not attend – that the church is a vibrant part of the community with something relevant to say and the imagination to present it creatively.

- Phone newsroom of local press and radio stations to give brief outline of event and invite them to cover it. (Ensure that you obtain a contact name and can start to build a relationship with that person.)

- Follow this with brief written details or call in to see the reporter in person. Offer interviews with the event chairperson or director.

- If local reporters decide not to cover the event themselves, send a press release containing the who, what, why, when, where and how of the event. (Remember to confirm all public statements with the chairperson.) Follow up with a phone call to check the reporter has all they need. (Note that press releases to radio and television stations should not be sent more than a week and a half ahead of the event.)

- Send details to local community and church bulletins.

- Send details to programme presenters of "What's on" features on local radio and television.

- If reporters do not cover the event, send a short report following the performance to your contact on the local papers. Include photograph if possible.

Box Office Ticketing Officer

Arrange for the printing and selling of the right number of tickets.

- Agree seating plan with house manager.

- Agree ticket pricing with chairperson.

- Agree print copy with chairperson and pass to publicity officer for printing.

- Decide distribution system – agents in churches, local Christian bookshop?

- Ensure that numbers of tickets sold and any money received or spent is accurately recorded.

- Monitor how many tickets are being sold.

- Bank the income regularly by arrangement with the treasurer.

Church Liaison Officer

Make contacts in the churches – clergy or lay as appropriate – and create enthusiasm about the event leading to effective support.

- Enthuse contacts to promote the event and encourage bookings.

- Encourage prayer support – corporately in church gatherings, and privately.

- Keep contacts informed as the project develops.

- Arrange for items in church magazines and arrange for pulpit announcements – provide draft notices.

- Liaise with publicity distributor to ensure a continuing supply of material.

- Explain the potential for bringing fringe or non-Christian friends – encourage the purchase of tickets for friends.

- Encourage party bookings.

Treasurer

Keep careful and accurate track of income and expenditure. Ensure that all involved with receiving and paying out money do so within the agreed policy and budget.

- Liaise with chairperson.

- Ensure all receipts due are collected, and all expenditure is claimed properly.
- Monitor actual transactions against budget.
- Operate a bank account.
- Compile accounts.

The following two roles will obviously only be needed if you decide to provide a meal during the evening.

Caterer

Provide meal with flair, enthusiasm and economy.

- Prepare workable menu costed and agreed with treasurer and chairperson.
- Agree timetable.
- Agree drinks list – imaginative non-alcoholic?
- Identify facilities.
- Identify cooking and ancillary volunteers.

Head Waiter

Responsible for the presentation of the food and drink to the guests.

- Work out logistics – number of tables – number of waiters – drinks stewards, etc.
- Agree with caterer how tables are decorated.
- Recruit appropriate waiters and drinks stewards – maybe from youth groups?
- Agree "uniform".
- Exercise discipline on the night – watch for delays, sloppy presentation. If the kitchen delays a course – explain to guests. Keep everyone happy.

Curtain Up: Notes on Performance
by Les Padfield

These notes were written to accompany the sketches that formed the *Entertaining Angels* revue, performed for the first time on Saturday 12 January 1995 at St Mildred's Church in South East London, by actors from Christ Church, Bromley, and South Lee Christian Centre. Brief notes for the Open Book sketches, commissioned in 1998, are contained before each script in that section.

The thought behind writing these notes is that they may be of some value to any future productions of the revue. Some or all of the ideas may be improved upon or rejected out-of-hand by future directors who see the sketches in a different light. Certainly the first production is not the definitive one. But it is in the hope that they may act as a springboard into new ideas that they are offered.

Staging

Our first plan for the revue was to do it in the round, with the actors sitting at tables among the audience, leaving and returning as their particular sketch began and finished. We felt that this kind of informality would enhance the relaxed and friendly spirit of the evening. It would also help the sense that performers and audience alike would learn from the revue. On a practical level, it meant the performers would also get fed that evening!

Playing in the round obviously has the problems of performing to both sides, and for some sketches this would have been especially difficult. Eventually we decided to revert to playing out, with the stage in front of the chancel and the audience seated all around the body of the church.

However, we kept to another original decision which was to have two stages, joined by a bridge (we used some smaller gymnasium benches). Our singers fitted snugly into a space behind one stage. As a result, we had the following pattern:

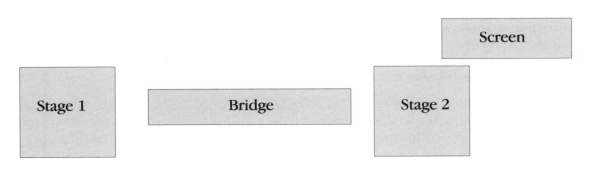

Audience

The thinking behind this arrangement was, firstly, that some of the sketches lent themselves to using two stages to create a kind of separation ("Tell Me More", "Two Women") and, secondly, two stages could be prepared simultaneously and so, ensure smooth scene changing and continuity. Overall, both reasons seemed justified when it came to performance. Props were minimal; scenery non-existent; and costume varied from sketch to sketch.

Angel Prep (Stage 1)

This opening sketch is vital in that it introduces the theme of angels which gives the play its title and continuity, and, more importantly, suggests there is a book – that humans have and angels don't – which explains the reason for life and God's relationship with his creation. In this way, the sketch sets the scene for the rest of the performance.

The script suggests Nova as a schoolteacher figure with perhaps a mortar-board, but our Nova was less authoritarian. Giving Nova a light-coloured suit, bow tie, gown and clipboard, we tried to combine the angel and educational sides of his persona. He had the freedom of both stages – though he actually spoke from the bridge – and the licence to ad lib a little if he saw people in the audience whom he could address directly in his opening speech. Because of this, we cut out a few of the individual comments on the "pupils" contained in the script. Another alteration was that "Dennis" became "Denise" in our version. When instructing Denise, Nova summoned up on the screen behind Stage 2 a picture of the earth, and this disappeared again on cue at the end of the piece when he pointed to it.

The Cookbook (Stage 2 – already set up before the opening)

This is quite a long and potentially static monologue, so it was necessary for a few props to be employed – cooking utensils, wine, bags of sugar and flour, and a stale loaf of bread. The cook – who spoke in a French accent – began confidently and gradually deteriorated both in his facial expressions and physical co-ordination, as he made a mess with the flour, discarded his chef's hat, and finally sank on to the stool in a pathetic heap, knocking off the table the cookbook that had been there. For a bit of humour we had him cutting the bread firstly with a knife, then an electric knife, and then with a bow saw. (We removed the kitchen table at the end of the sketch and replaced it with the salesman's desk, whilst Stage 1 was simultaneously prepared for the Revd Wakey in "The Jesus Shop".)

The Jesus Shop (Stage 1); Selling Out (Stage 2)

These two sketches make similar points about misusing the Bible, so we ran them seamlessly one after the other. As "The Jesus Shop" blacked out on Stage 1, "Selling Out" began on Stage 2. Our gullible client in "The Jesus Shop" was a woman not a man, which made little difference except that we changed a few brothers to sisters. We also beamed up a picture of the Patron (ours was a Mr R Maxwell, though more contemporary patrons for today could easily be imagined!).

As it is quite a long monologue, "Selling Out" needed some visual interest, so we incorporated a secretary who brought in coffee and biscuits and rather distracted the salesman for a few moments. A (mock) mobile phone is essential here for any movement. (At the end Stage 1 can be cleared to become "Nottingham" in "Tell Me More", whilst Stage 2 is simply changed from the salesman's desk to the TV presenters' table.)

Tell Me More (Stages 1 and 2)

We made some radical changes here, re-sexing a number of characters. Staging was done with three presenters on Stage 1 – two girls and one man – then cutting to Stage 2 for the interviews in Nottingham. Because John (who changed to Fiona) was somehow meant to be in Nottingham and back in the studio, we invented a new presenter and left John (Fiona) to do only the interviews. We decided to add a bit of muscle to Anna, the "real" Christian in the sketch, and turned her into Alan, who was weight-lifting at the local gym when he was interviewed. He came across as dead straight, and his final answer obviously embarrasses the rather superior interviewer.

To balance out the sexes, we then changed George the verger into Doris the cleaner, leaving the Revd Pickles to be himself. A few bars of *Blue Peter* music at the start and end of the sketch might not go amiss. (Changing to Stage 2 for the next sketch meant that we didn't have to clear away the props until the interval, which enhanced continuity.)

The Book of Fish (Stage 1)

Very little direction was needed here as the sketch rests entirely on its characters and their delivery.

Link to and from the interval (Bridge)

Nova returned at this point, and told the assembled angels just how to organise themselves for the meal. He could perhaps say grace, and make any other announcements before the meal. At the appropriate moment he returned to give quiz answers and instructed the assembled "angels" to settle down for the second half.

The Rediscovery of the Bible (Stage 2)

We felt that it would be good to bring variation to the evening, and so for this sketch we used our local technical genius to pre-record the News summary and all of the interviews, which were then shown on the screen. This allowed us a bit of fun as he was able to incorporate *News at Ten* intro music, and place Kevin Ethics in different situations. Arthur Streebly acquired a Germanic lilt to his voice and a 'von' in front of his surname; the futuristic Archbishop was a woman interviewed outside the Rose and Crown in Watford.

In the middle of the sketch we cut to "real life" and had our two anglers on stage, sitting fishing in a small boat, with a picture of lapping water on the screen behind.

The Bible that they rediscover became the visible motif for the second half – the same (fairly distinctive) copy emerging in each of the sketches after the interval.

Beginning with "J"

This sketch was not written until after the first performance. Some suggestions on performance, written by the author, appear together with the sketch itself on page 46.

Two Women (Stages 1 and 2)

The same Bible as in "The Rediscovery of the Bible" reappears, read by the man who is positioned on the bridge in this sketch. The women took up positions, one on either stage, which allowed for Woman 1 to be blacked out on the words "switched off", leaving light only on the Man (God) and Woman 2.

Philip and the Ethiopian (Stages 1 and 2)

This sketch immediately suggested to us the idea of clowns. Though we risked objections from the purists, we dressed the two actors accordingly, and had them juggling (badly) for a few seconds before they noticed the audience. The humour of the sketch is so strong that it's difficult not to perform it successfully. The clown idea allowed a lot of movement, from one stage to another, and we hired a chauffeur to drive the eunuch around the stage before pulling in at a lay-by. Once more the same Bible appeared, read upside-down by the eunuch!

The Five-minute Bible (Stages 1 and 2 and auditorium)

Denise preceded this sketch by rushing on with that now familiar Bible, which was then passed to Nova for the last lines of the whole evening.

"The Five Minute Bible" sketch itself was written for four actors, but we employed twenty-three! Originally we decided that it would be good to finish the evening with some kind of audience participation – not to be gimmicky, but more as a slightly symbolic gesture that the evening was intended to involve them and to be more than a performance. We planned, therefore, to involve all our actors, partly because we wanted everyone included, and also because it would have been a real killer for only four people to learn. Lines were shared out, and the first idea was to have the actors sitting on the edge of the stage, rising to deliver their lines, and returning to sit again. Having spoken their last individual lines, they were then going to walk back to their seats in the audience for the final "Come Lord Jesus" and "Amen" lines.

The organisation of this, however, with the trafficking of actors this would involve, led us to decide instead on starting with the actors in their seats and delivering the lines from these positions. This meant putting the house lights up and having voices coming from all over the church. On stage we had Denise and Nova miming a few of the lines (Adam and Eve; the killing of Cain, with a cap gun; the slaying of Goliath, with a whistle and a red card; and the crucifixion of Jesus). As each book of the Bible was mentioned, its name was projected on to the screen behind the actors, finally merging into the two words "The Bible".

All the cast sang "The Battle of Jericho", joined in announcing "The New Testament" and "the Church is born" and then, having spoken their final individual lines came forward to the front of the stage to form a line with Nova, Denise and the Boy on the Bridge behind. On the final "Come Lord Jesus" they raised hands, Nova read the penultimate line from "The Bible", and a very solid "Amen" took the lights off.

This made for a striking and very effective ending. If others were to adopt it, I would strongly recommend the avoidance of any additional "sermon" or thank yous to round the evening off. A sample programme appears on page 22.

Of Flyers and Programmes
by Kim Brown and Lindsay Shaw

From old-fashioned gossip to hi-tech websites, there are all kinds of ways of getting word around about your *Entertaining Angels* event. One important item in your publicity armoury will be the printed flyer. In order to give a distinct visual identity for the event and to get its humour across, we have designed and included a flyer which you can overprint with details of your venue, date and so on. Both sides of this A5 flyer are contained on the following page. For the person who will arrange the printing of these materials, we have also included some technical details below.

In addition to the flyer, we have included a programme master to print from and to customise with details of your venue, performers and production team. The programme order is one we would recommend, though you are free to adapt or shorten it as you wish.

For all types of printing: enlarging the masters

To fit within the binding of this book, the flyer and programme masters have both been reduced to 90% of an A4 sheet. To litho print from them you will need to enlarge them by 11% to a finished image size of 297 x 120 mm (image bleeds all edges). To photocopy from them use them at the size supplied and centre the image on the finished sheet.

Photocopying

Best results will be obtained if you copy in black only on to tinted papers. Pastel shades are recommended, as strong colours will overwhelm the design. The master we have provided for the flyer has been produced "two up" (one front and one back) while the programme has been produced "one up". When you copy these on to double-sided paper, place the masters manually rather than use the automatic document feed. Ensure the flyer will back correctly with the text on each side the same way up. Copy the master on to both sides of your A4 sheets. With the flyer, you should then cut copies in half to give separate A5 flyers.

Litho printing in single colour

Use strong ink colours (preferably dark blue, dark purple, deep red or dark orange), taking care to avoid colour clash if you choose a tinted paper. Follow other guidance given above.

Two-colour litho printing

Use a strong ink colour for the text (see above) and choose a second colour that complements it and does not clash with the paper colour. Use a good quality printer and ensure that the colours "fit" together (there are no white areas where colours should butt to each other). Recommended colours: orange and mid-blue ink; white paper (matt).

Customising artwork

Venue, date, time and ticket price (if applicable) should be typeset in a sans serif, roman face and positioned in the box provided on the master. Ensure that the text is large enough to be read easily. There is space on the back for you to add details of the churches staging the event. For the programme, venue details (on page 1) and performers and production team details (on page 4) can be added in a clear sans serif face in the spaces available.

BIBLE SOCIETY

presents

Entertaining Angels

An evening of laughter, satire and enlightenment designed to entertain and challenge

With music by Michael Card

Entertaining Angels

by Stephen Deal
John Duckworth
Bridget Foreman
Steve Newman
Les Padfield
Nick Page
Adrian Plass

A highly original evening that shows the Bible as it really is – surprising, relevant, vibrant – and brought to life through sketches, music and song.

No wings required – just reserve your ticket now for this unique event staged by a talented cast from local churches.

Join Dennis, a junior angel, on an enlightening, laughter- and satire - filled quest for the truth about the universe, humans and a brilliant little book that might possibly have something to say to them.

The Open Book

Bible Society, Stonehill Green, Westlea, SWINDON SN5 7DG
Tel: 01793 418100. Fax: 01793 418118
Charity Registration No. 232759

Entertaining Angels

An evening of laughter, satire and enlightenment designed to entertain and challenge.

Day

Date

Time

Venue

The Cast

The Band

The Production

Director:

Assistant director:

Musical director:

Lighting:

Props:

Staging team:

Catering:

Bible Society

Bible Societies exist to provide resources for Bible distribution and use. The British and Foreign Bible Society (BFBS) is a member of the United Bible Societies, an international partnership working in over 180 countries. Their common aim is to reach all people with the Bible, or some part of it, in a language they can understand and at a price they can afford.

Stonehill Green, Westlea,
Swindon, SN5 7DG, England
Website: www.biblesociety.org.uk
Tel. 01793 418100; Fax 01793 413113
e-mail info@bfbs.org.uk.

The Open Book

BIBLE SOCIETY

Entertaining Angels

The authors

Stephen Deal is a writer. He was a founder member of Stripes Theatre Company and has written extensively for the Rob Frost Organisation. He has also written sketches for television.

Bridget Foreman is a director and writer. She is an Artistic Associate of Riding Lights Theatre company, for whom her full-length plays include *A Dangerous Game*, *A Different Drum* and *Barking Up the Christmas Tree*.

Steve Newman is an actor, writer and musician. He has appeared in *Me and My Girl* at the Adelphi Theatre and has written the definitive football musical *Only Heroes Dribble*.

Les Padfield is a teacher at a London Secondary School and Director of Drama at Christchurch, Bromley. He directed the first performance of *Entertaining Angels*.

Nick Page is a writer and was a founder member of Ambush Theatre Company. He is now Head of the Media Department at the Oasis Trust. His latest book is *The Tabloid Bible*.

Adrian Plass is a best-selling author of eighteen books including his *Sacred Diary*. As a speaker, he presents his unique brand of humour, poetry and storytelling in venues as varied as prisons and theatres and contributes regularly to national and local radio and television.

The songwriter

Michael Card is an award-winning songwriter and recording artist, best-known for the song *El Shaddai*. His albums include two trilogies, one based on the life of Christ and the other on the Old Testament. He lives in rural Tennessee.

First half

The Bible: What? Why? Who? How?
Tackling some current questions about the Bible

Why was the Bible written?

Angel Prep by Stephen Deal
Dennis's quest begins . . .

So Many Books by Michael Card
The hunger for God's Word

How is the Bible misused?

The Jesus Shop by Steve Newman
The dangers of using verses out of context

Selling Out by Bridget Foreman
The Bible and consumerism

Scandalon by Michael Card
The scandal of believing

What ideas do people have about the Bible?

Tell Me More by Bridget Foreman
Some current attitudes

Could it Be? by Michael Card
The key to believing is a person

How is the Bible relevant?

The Book of Fish by Stephen Deal
Some ways the Bible is criticised

Second half

The Bible Bites Back
Stories of hope and change

So Many Books (reprise) by Michael Card

The Rediscovery of the Bible by Nick Page
(2 Kings 22—23; 2 Chronicles 34)
The Bible was lost before. How might it happen again?

That's What Faith Must Be by Michael Card
God's presence and guidance in human lives

Beginning with "J" by Adrian Plass
(John 6.5—13; Acts 20.7—12)
The amazing results of a personal encounter with Jesus

The Final Word by Michael Card
God's thoughts put into a human life

Two Women by Les Padfield
(Luke 18.9—14)
Contrasting God's view of people and our own

Philip and the Ethiopian by Nick Page
(Acts 8.26—39)
How the Bible can have a lasting effect on someone's life

Joy in the Journey by Michael Card
The exhilaration of the life of faith

The Five-Minute Bible by Stephen Deal
Dennis finds the book he has been looking for . . . .

Sketches for the Entertaining Angels Revue

Angel Prep
by Stephen Deal

CAST

NOVA

DENNIS

House lights are up. An angel (Nova) wearing an academic gown and mortar board enters. He carries a pile of exercise books. He addresses the audience as if they are his class. Somewhere in the audience Dennis is located.

NOVA: Stand when I enter the room. Have we forgotten our manners, class 4B?

(Nova waits until the audience is standing.)

That's better. You may sit.

I have here the essays you handed in last lesson. You may well look anxious Jenkins Minor. "Predestination and free will – The paradox explained."

(Nova goes into the audience to distribute the pile of exercise books. As each name is called out he hands or throws an exercise book to that member of the audience. A degree of ad libbing may be necessary to keep control of the "class".)

Harris, B minus, a good effort. Farnham, B plus, excellent work boy. Crowley, C, very average. I'd hoped for better. Lewis, look at the state of this exercise book boy. I do not expect cherubs in my class to hand in work in this condition. Re-cover this book, it's disgusting. *(He holds the book very carefully by the corner and drops it into someone's lap.)* Stanwick, C plus, you're improving. Cavendish, C plus, this would have been a B but for some silly grammatical errors. Glenn, D, very shoddy. Jenkins Minor, E, do it again. Stephens, B, not bad. Catch. *(He throws the book across the room.)* Don't whimper boy, it only caught you on the nose. It'll stop bleeding soon. You should pay more attention. Foswick, A plus, top of the class, well done. Nicely reasoned and beautifully phrased. Stand up boy, let everyone see you.

(Nova indicates to a member of the audience to stand.) Look at this cherub class. This is the third time this term he's handed in the best essay. I think he deserves a clap, don't you.

(Waits for audience to clap.) You're going to make a fine angel one day, a fine angel. Right, where were we? Peterson, C minus, you're slipping. Read my comments carefully and you may just scrape through your exam at the end of term . . . but I doubt it. Jenkins Minor, stop whispering to Glenn. If you have something to say, say it out loud so we can all join in. Well, I'm waiting . . . See me after class and we can discuss it then. And, finally, Whitechapel, a rather surprising B, well done indeed.

(He throws out the last book and returns to the stage.)

Well what can I say? With one or two notable exceptions a pretty pathetic effort. Does this class wish to remain cherubs for ever? Don't you wish to attain the giddy heights of angelhood? If you do you'd better knuckle down and see if you can make some improvements. So, without further ado, let us embark upon the exercise of enlightenment.

(He stares around the "class" and notices Dennis *for the first time.)*

NOVA: You boy.

DENNIS: Please, sir?

NOVA: Yes, you boy, stand up.

           (Dennis stands.)

NOVA: Ah! You must be the new cherub.

DENNIS: Yes sir.

NOVA: Well, do you have a name cherub?

DENNIS: Yes sir, Dennis, sir.

NOVA: Dennis. And do you have any questions, Dennis?

DENNIS: No sir.

NOVA: Oh come now. Surely you have at least one question, and this is the place to ask it.

DENNIS: The universe, the heavens, life. There must be a purpose to it all. But what is it? What's it all about?

NOVA: Well, I was expecting something a little more prosaic like "where are the toilets", but . . . A surprisingly pertinent question from one so . . . so . . . unkempt. Straighten your tie and come out here boy. Quickly now, chop, chop.

           (As Dennis makes his way to the stage the house lights go down and the stage lights come up. Ideally a picture of planet earth should be projected on to the stage.)

NOVA: This, Dennis, is what it's all about. Planet earth, the jewel of creation.

DENNIS: It's very pretty, but why is it so special?

NOVA: Do you believe in humans, Dennis?

DENNIS: Well sort of, I suppose. I've never really thought about it. Do you sir?

NOVA: Yes I do, Dennis. But, more importantly, so does the Creator. He believes in humans so much he has nurtured and protected them, encouraged and disciplined them, walked with them and even died for them.

DENNIS: But why?

NOVA: I could answer that question for you, Dennis, but I'm a teacher and you are a pupil. Think how much more satisfying it would be for you to find out through your own efforts.

DENNIS: I wouldn't know where to start.

NOVA: Well, let me see. You'd want to know about the relationship that has been forged between the Creator and his creation. You'd want to get a sense of how that relationship has been tried and tested over the generations. So you'd want to examine the agreements and covenants that have been formed and see how they affect individuals and entire countries. That means you'd want to study the case histories of prominent figures and read up on the major events in the history of key nations. Then you'd need to see if the relationship has been damaged and find out what has been done to mend it. And finally you'd want to come to an understanding of how the relationship can be maintained and developed

DENNIS: I'll never be able to find all that out.

NOVA: Yes you will. Go to the library and start work.

DENNIS: But it'll take for ever.

NOVA: Very possibly.

DENNIS: It'll take ages just to find all the relevant books to read.

NOVA: No doubt.

DENNIS: Isn't there just one book I could read?

NOVA: Cherubs today! You want everything handed to you on a plate. Just one book indeed. You ask the question "What's it all about?" and you expect the answer to be neatly summed up in just one book.

DENNIS: But imagine if there was such a book. Everyone would want to read it.

NOVA: Well they'd be rather foolish if they didn't.

DENNIS: It would be brilliant if there were a little book where you could at least start looking for the answers.

NOVA: Yes, but since there isn't you'd better start work in the library.

DENNIS: I wonder how the humans manage. After all, they haven't got our library.

NOVA: I'm sure the Creator has thought of that.

DENNIS: Perhaps he's given them my book . . . And sir?

NOVA: Yes Dennis?

DENNIS: There is one more question I'd like to ask.

NOVA: Down the corridor, on the left.

DENNIS: Thank you sir.

NOVA: And the library is further down on the right.

DENNIS: Thank you sir.

I Don't Read the Cookbook Any More

Based on the story "I Don't Read the Cookbook Any More"

From *Stories that Sneak Up on You* by John Duckworth
(Fleming H Revell, a division of Baker Book House © 1987)

CAST

COOK

On stage there is a table with a bag of flour, a bag of sugar, a jug of water, a mixing bowl, a wooden spoon, and a rolling pin. The cook enters wearing an apron, and stares at the ingredients in a rather puzzled way.

COOK: I don't read the Cookbook any more. I know some people say you should read it all the time, especially when you're going to cook something. But that sort of thing isn't really me.

When I first became a cook, I read the Cookbook all the time. In fact, before I became a cook I loved reading the recipes, and wondered if I could bake and fry and make all those delicious-sounding dishes. Then I got to the part of the Cookbook that tells you how to become a cook, and I went right ahead and followed the directions. I remember being so happy.

During those first months I practically always had the Cookbook with me wherever I went. People would ask me what the book was and why I was carrying it with me; I'd be able to tell them how I'd just become a cook. I was so excited, I wanted everyone else to start cooking too.

After a few years, though, I didn't study the Cookbook as much. I mean, I'd got pretty good at this cooking lark now. I'd made most things from beef Stroganoff to baked Alaska, and they'd turned out quite well. Once in a while I'd accidentally skip an ingredient or use a whisk incorrectly and the meal would be a bit of a disaster. But I was getting quite a reputation as a cook and I really didn't need to read the Cookbook so much.

I gave up reading a portion of the cooking instructions each day, so much of it was boring especially the first two-thirds, which was the history of cooking and how they used to do things in the old days. Who needs that, I asked myself. This is now. We've got microwaves and food processors – not brick ovens.

Besides I just didn't have enough time for it, I was so busy being a good cook that I really couldn't be expected to read and reread my Cookbook as well!

Next I tried cooking something without reading the recipe first. I whipped up a chocolate cake without even glancing at the Cookbook, and do you know – it turned out OK. So before long I was making more complicated recipes without the Cookbook, things like soufflés and duck a l'orange. Sometimes I had never read the recipes at all, but I'd definitely heard a lecture about them once. And in some cases I hadn't actually heard a lecture but I reckoned I knew enough about cooking by now to have a go.

I got quite good at substituting ingredients and guessing at baking temperatures, although I have to admit that some of the results weren't exactly the sort of thing you'd take to the bring-and-buy sale. Eventually I couldn't remember many of the recipes, so I began to invent my own. They were fairly close to the originals, but I couldn't be absolutely sure because I seemed to have lost my Cookbook somewhere. Some people weren't too keen on the dishes I'd invented – savoury sponge cake for instance – but I didn't care. What was I supposed to do anyway – memorise recipes?

A few of my cooking friends even criticised me, saying I ought to read the Cookbook more. I tried to calm them down by buying a brand new copy, a big one edged in gold. I took it to cooking-society meetings, and made sure everyone noticed it. But I didn't open it, of course.

I *did* read cooking-related books – about stoves, and diets, and grocery shopping. Some of those were quite interesting – which is more than I could say for the Cookbook itself.

Gradually, I got rather fed up with my fellow cooks pestering me to get "back into my Cookbook", and so I went to cooking-society meetings less and less. When a friend asked me about this, I told her I regularly watched one of the cooking shows on the telly. And I did – for a while.

These days I don't do much cooking. If I get really hungry, I warm up something in the microwave. Once in a while I might get into a spot of bother and have to whip up a batch of scones, but the old zeal just isn't there any more.

If I bump into any of my old cooking friends these days I know they're thinking – "I bet she can't even remember how to boil water."

What would they know! Of *course* I can remember how to boil water. I just can't remember *why*.

The Jesus Shop
by Steve Newman

CAST

WIDE BOY

MAN

Wide boy type character wearing a dog collar on stage – man enters.

WIDE BOY: Lovely mornin' squire.

MAN: Hello, is this the "Jesus Shop"?

WIDE BOY: Correct squire, sit down, I'm Reverend Wakey – so you're interested in our Jesus Insurance Policy?

MAN: Sounds very good.

WIDE BOY: Certainly is brother, now let me explain; as you know most insurance policies stop when you're dead – this one doesn't – in fact the premium you pay now will be paid out at the end of eternity – "store your treasures in heaven" as our patron says.

MAN: How long will that be then?

WIDE BOY: Like I said near the end of time, that is to say, near enough to the end of time to allow enough time at the other end to spend it! Look, a thousand years is but a couple of ticks in the place of many maisonettes.

MAN: So what happens when I die?

WIDE BOY: All that you've contributed in this life will be up there waiting for you – "your reward shall be great in heaven", see? Now how much can you afford?

MAN: Not much, I'm unemployed at the moment.

WIDE BOY: "Blessed are the poor" brother, so where ist thy dwelling place?

MAN: My mum and dad's.

WIDE BOY: "Honour thy Father and Mother", nice one. What about possessions? As our patron once said "Sell all you have and give it to the poor".

MAN: But I am poor!

WIDE BOY: And "the poor will always be with us" – you lucky man, the poorer you are in this life means the wealthier you'll be in the heavenlies – it's logical isn't it?

MAN: Well I do have a car.

WIDE BOY: Elijah's winged chariot.

MAN: It's an Astra actually.

WIDE BOY: What about your mum? Has she any spare cash lying around? Remember "They had all things in common, sharing everything from the common purse."

MAN: What? Steal from my mum?

WIDE BOY: "Let your right hand not know what your left one is doing." Anyway brother, she would be merely "casting her bread upon the water of life which will return to her ten fold" at some future unspecified date when you can afford the interest!

MAN: But then she might chuck me out, I'd be homeless.

WIDE BOY: "I have nowhere to lay my head, even the foxes have their nests" – Look squire, put all your money with us and "you'll lighten your load, you'll get through the eye of the needle", you'll be free indeed – "even when you walk through the valley of the six hundred you will find yourself by the rivers of Babylon, under the tree of Shalom, stuffing your face with heavenly manna!"

MAN: It sounds too good to be true.

WIDE BOY: Such is the large beating heart of our patron – sign here and "gifts will pour from heaven on to your head" – and you'll get a free biro with our logo on it – well done. "Your name is now writ in the Book of Celestial Time Share Properties" – congratulations!

MAN: Well, I feel better for that.

WIDE BOY: Course you do, "your burden is lifted", "we set the captives free", well, bye for now Squire.

MAN: I don't know how to thank you.

WIDE BOY: No need squire, as our motto says "We saw a stranger and we took him in!" Or as the good book says "there ist one borneth every minute".

MAN: Does the good book really say that?

WIDE BOY: *(Really worried.)* Oh . . . hast thou ever read it my son?

MAN: No, I'm afraid I haven't.

WIDE BOY: Well then, of course it does squire, oh yes indeed. All the best son, Bye. *(Exit Man.)*

Selling Out
by Bridget Foreman

CAST

SIMON

Simon is on the phone in a telesales office. Simon is a confident and practised salesman, who gives the impression of having a genuine enthusiasm for the product as well as a real interest in the opinions of the person he is speaking to. However, much of the horror of his character comes not only from his attitude towards the Bible, but also his glib compartmentalisation of other people.

SIMON: Hello, is this Reverend Moose? . . . Oh, Moore. Oh, I am sorry, Reverend Moore, my secretary's handwriting is dreadful.

Hello. My name's Simon Bishop – Discovery Publications – I expect you've heard of us.

No? . . . Well, I always say that we aim to reclaim – to blow the dust off the treasures of yesteryear – to draw aside the curtain of time that separates us from the wisdom of ages past . . .

Yes, well, the point I am getting to, Reverend Moore, is that we are handling a very exciting project at the moment, and we'd like to invite you to share in it. We believe that you could play a crucial role by endorsing our new range of products. It will just take a few minutes to explain . . . *(Hollow laugh.)* . . . Yes, I'm sure we'll be through before your communion service on Sunday – something of a comedian, eh, Reverend?

Now, let me ask you a question. Do you think it would be fair to say that the Bible is a greatly neglected book in our society? . . .

Yes, I knew you'd agree. Would you like to hazard a guess as to why that is? . . . *(Long pause – the Revd has evidently embarked on a sermon.)*

Yes . . . um . . . Yes, well, that's very philosophical, but I'm going to have to put you right there, Reverend.

Marketing. It's as simple as that.

The Bible has never been properly promoted – it's never been targeted at the right market . . . That's absolutely right, Reverend, until now.

How did you know I was going to say that? Not just a comedian, but a prophet too, eh? *(He laughs rather too much at his own joke.)* . . . Yes, of course.

Well, Discovery Publications has come up with an ingenious repackaging strategy that will put the bite back into the Bible . . . No, I suppose a shark wouldn't need a set of dentures.

There's no getting anything past you, is there, Reverend Moore?

But give me a chance – here's an example: imagine for a moment that you are an environmentalist. You ride a bicycle. You use eco-friendly washing

31

powder. You vote for the Green Party. You recycle your empty elderflower wine bottles.

You want a spiritual peg to hang your beliefs on. And Discovery Publications gives it to you: the creation story, hand-printed on recycled paper, and with a free astrology chart, for just £11.99.

Did you know that Genesis gives a charter for vegetarianism? Astonishing! And so relevant. We're far too hasty these days in abandoning the accumulated knowledge of former generations. And we're all trying to do our bit for the environment, aren't we? I expect you've even been known to recycle the odd sermon, eh?

(He laughs, but evidently receives a put-down from Revd Moore.) . . . Yes, well, you know what they say, the old ones are the best.

But check this out: suppose that I am terribly socially aware. I read the *Guardian*. I drive a 2CV. I give my old clothes to a hostel for battered women. I buy my coffee from Oxfam. I need some reassurance that the social injustices of the world will somehow be lighted.

And Discovery Publications gives it to me for just £15.00: a coffee-table edition of the beatitudes, with full-colour photographs from around the world. On one page the words "blessed are you who are poor, for yours is the kingdom of God", on the facing page, a photograph of a small black child sitting under a water pump, and laughing as the water cascades over him.

What do you think of that? . . . Over-simplification? . . . Not at all. It's a matter of style: feel good consumer targeting. This is what people want. And our new abbreviated Bibles make the most superb gifts.

We anticipate that our lovers' edition of the Song of Solomon will be a best-seller. This really is a very special product: hand-bound on pure vellum, with gilt-edged, scented pages, this comes in a his or hers gift pack that includes either a pair of silk boxer shorts in a range of colours, or a luxury satin negligée. And that will set you back just £36.99.

You see – there really is something in the Bible for everyone, and Discovery Publications has increased the Bible's appeal by eliminating what's irrelevant.

We give people the essentials . . . well, it's admirable that you find the whole thing indispensable, but believe me, Reverend, you are in the minority: our market research indicates that the whole Bible carries a high negativity rating . . .

Yes, I can appreciate that breaking those barriers down must be a very difficult but essential part of your job, but our products are designed to help you in that . . .

I don't see how they could possibly be a hindrance – what exactly do you mean by that? . . . Yup . . . uh-huh . . . Well, that's a very interesting viewpoint, Reverend.

So, will you consider endorsing our products, and helping people to discover the relevance of the Bible? . . .

I'm sorry? . . .

Me? . . .

Well, I don't think I've personally ever found any parts of it particularly relevant . . .

It's just not my style, y'know? . . .

Jesus? . . .

Yeah, he was a good bloke, but that's as far as it goes . . . *(Laughs.)* . . .

You're not suggesting that anyone these days really believes all that Son of God stuff.

I think civilisation's moved on a bit from that, don't you?

Tell Me More
by Bridget Foreman

CAST

SARAH – Presenter

JOHN – Presenter

LORRAINE – Presenter

GEORGE – Verger

ANTONY – Vicar

ANNA – Young woman

Sarah, John and Lorraine are presenters of Tell Me More, *a worthy and informative television programme for children. They are to some extent blank pieces of paper on which media personalities can be drawn to a greater or lesser degree. George, the verger, is elderly and preoccupied, and may well be helped by some kind of regional accent. Antony, the vicar, is middle class, affable and patronising, and in contrast Anna should be played as straight and honestly as is possible.*

The sketch needs to be taken at some pace: much of the humour is of the "throwaway" variety, and will benefit from a light, deft style of performance. The making of the Bible should be enacted fully, and for real, i.e. using real honey, etc.

SARAH:
Hello, and welcome again to *Tell Me More*. This week we conclude our series of special reports on the Bible. John is in Nottingham to find out who is reading it and why. John.

JOHN:
Yes, I'm here at St Martin's church and I'm going to try to find out a little bit more about the Bible. *(He approaches a muttering figure.)* This is George Mountford, the verger. George, can you tell us what you know about the Bible?

GEORGE:
I'll tell you what I know about the Bible. I know that people never leave them the right way up in the pews. If I had a penny for every time I've had to sort out this mess, I'd be a rich man. People come in here, they pick them up, they read them a bit and just put them down willy-nilly. They don't seem to realise that it matters which way up you leave them.

JOHN:
So, do you feel that people have lost their reverence for the Bible?

GEORGE:
Oh, yes. Oh, it's terrible. You wouldn't believe how badly some people treat their Bibles – they read them so much that they get tatty and dog-eared, some people even write in them and underline their favourite bits. And worst of all, they let their children get hold of them – even here, in church – you wouldn't credit it. On occasions, I've even had to wrestle Bibles out of the hands of toddlers.

JOHN:
The Bible obviously plays a large part in your life, then?

GEORGE:
Large part? My life revolves around the blinking things. *(He wanders off, muttering.)*

JOHN:	Moving on, I'm speaking now to the Reverend Antony Pickles. Antony, you're the vicar here.
ANTONY:	That's right.
JOHN:	Antony, could you tell us what you think the Bible can offer people?
ANTONY:	I think that first and foremost it's a great source of spiritual encouragement. I know of many people who've been very cheered by reading the Bible when they've been feeling under the weather.
JOHN:	Why do you think that is?
ANTONY:	Well, I think it's the language, really. It lifts you right out of everyday life, and takes you to another world. It's very important that people have some form of escapism, and I think the Bible gives that. It's also got lots of soothing, calming stuff in it.
JOHN:	Isn't some of it very violent?
ANTONY:	Well, yes . . .
JOHN:	It has been alleged that the Bible is a very tough, uncompromising book.
ANTONY:	I try to leave out the nastier bits. Generally, I tell people to try a nice psalm before bed.
JOHN:	Lastly, Anna Wilcox, you're a member of the congregation here. Why do you read the Bible?
ANNA:	It's the most interesting book I've ever read. It's exciting, it's challenging . . .
JOHN:	Isn't it rather complicated?
ANNA:	Well obviously I don't understand it all, but I don't think anybody does. I'm still learning.
JOHN:	What about all those "thees" and "thous"?
ANNA:	Actually, my Bible hasn't got any. It's just written in normal English.
JOHN:	Gosh, that's very up to date. I notice that your Bible has some photographs in it. Now, be honest with us, Anna, do you really read the Bible, or do you just look at the pictures?
ANNA:	I like the photographs – they help me to imagine what things were like when Jesus was around, but I do read the Bible too. Sometimes I like to pretend that I'm there, seeing everything happen.
JOHN:	Ooh, that sounds fun. So what's your answer to people who say the Bible is boring?
ANNA:	There are some difficult parts. But it's worth sticking at it. I find that God speaks to me through the Bible.
	(Awkward pause.)
JOHN:	Yes. *(Turns to camera.)* Well, there you have it. The Bible obviously means all kinds of different things to different people. One thing is

certain: for some reason it is the world's all-time best-selling book. Back to the studio.

LORRAINE: Yes, well, as we were hearing from John just now, the Bible is a best-seller. And now we're going to give you the chance to have your very own Bible. But you don't need to spend lots of money on one from the shops. I'm going to show you how to make one with some old cornflakes packets and a jar of honey.

Now, as we all know, the Bible is very boring. So I've cut some rectangles out of cereal boxes, that are going to be our pages. Glue them back to back so they're stiff and dull, and make sure that none of the interesting printed parts are showing. And if you do enough of these to make up about an inch-and-a-half in thickness, that will make up the main part of your Bible.

Now, about three-quarters of the way through comes Christmas. For this bit you'll need an old Christmas card. Here's mine. Cut off the back part – mine says "Buy yourself something smelly, love Aunty Marjorie" – but yours could say anything, and keep the front part with the picture on. This is a lovely one of a stable with a big star and lots of people looking at the baby. Now, just brush some honey over the card to make it sweet and sticky, and pop it in a low oven until it's half-baked.

While that's cooking, you've got time to cut out the bits that don't taste very nice. You may need to ask a liberal theologian to help you with this, and be careful not to leave any scraps lying around, as they could be dangerous.

Christmas should be just about done by now – here's one I prepared earlier – so pop it in between the boring parts. And to finish it off, spread a little more honey over the front cover and stick a few pressed flowers on it for Creation. And there you have it. Your very own Bible. Sarah.

SARAH: Finally, our competition results. We asked you to send in your suggestions for a *Tell Me More* book for the Bible. We have been inundated with ideas. We liked all your entries, but we could only choose three winners. In third place is Craig Morgan, aged nine. He sent us a wonderful parcel of Bible smells – a dead fish for the sea of Galilee, some camel dung for the stable at Bethlehem, and an apple core for the garden of Eden. Craig, we thought your smells might be a little difficult to integrate into the Bible, but we loved your idea, so the third prize of a set of *Tell Me More* pencils goes to you.

JOHN: In second place is Susannah Wilmot, aged twelve, who sent us a bumper pack of puzzles and word searches to make the Bible a little more stimulating, and to pass the time during boring sermons. And Susannah gets the second prize of the new *Tell Me More* computer game, "Tell Me Even More".

SARAH: But our overall winner is Emily Simons, aged eleven. Her winning entry is "The Big Book of Tell Me More Helpful Hints", and here are some of them:

36

LORRAINE: Be nice to animals.

JOHN: Recycle old coke cans.

SARAH: Use unleaded petrol.

LORRAINE: Always have a bring-and-buy sale to alleviate starvation in the third world.

JOHN: Give your lollipop lady an Easter egg.

SARAH: Invent an ironing machine for Mummy.

LORRAINE: And, amazingly, Emily came up with another 142 helpful hints. So, congratulations, Emily. Your book will go into the Bible in a month's time.

JOHN: Well, that's all for today, but do join us next week when I'll be climbing Mount Everest with just some string and a bag of dried apricots.

LORRAINE: And I'll be showing you how to make a sandwich out of a loaf of bread and some peanut butter.

ALL: Byeee!

The Book of Fish
by Stephen Deal

CAST

ERNEST

JOHN

John is sitting on a park bench reading his Bible and eating a packed lunch. Enter Ernest, who sits down next to John.

ERNEST: You don't mind if I sit here, do you?

JOHN: No, not at all.

ERNEST: Only I wouldn't want to disturb you.

JOHN: Thank you.

ERNEST: I can see that you are reading. I hate it when people disturb me when I'm reading. I find that most annoying . . . It's very irritating when people interrupt me when I'm reading a good book . . . Are you reading a good book?

JOHN: The Bible.

ERNEST: Not so much a good book as *the* Good Book. Ha ha. Just my little joke. Well then I *really* mustn't disturb you. I don't want to be struck by lightning. Ha ha.

JOHN: Thank you.

(They sit in silence, John *continues to read,* Ernest *starts to read over John's shoulder.)*

ERNEST: Good is it? The good book.

JOHN: Yes.

ERNEST: I've read a lot of books myself. There's nothing I like better than a good book. Not *the* good book you understand. Any good book. Personally, I don't think the Bible is a very good book. I find it very overrated.

JOHN: I'm sorry you feel that way. I find it very helpful.

ERNEST: Helpful! I've never found it helpful. Take for example the subject of goldfish.

JOHN: Goldfish.

ERNEST: Fascinating creatures, I think you'll agree. Did you know that the goldfish has the widest range of vision of any known creature. It can see all the way from infra-red to ultra-violet. I read that in a book. But that book was not the Bible.

JOHN: Really?

ERNEST: You won't read about goldfish in the Bible, did you know that?

JOHN: No.

ERNEST: The Bible is silent on the subject of goldfish. Goldfish are not deemed worthy of inclusion in the holy canon. You can scan the entire contents from cover to cover and not a word will you find pertaining to the common goldfish. I find that strange. After all if the Bible is the true word of God then you would have thought that goldfish would feature somewhere in it. They are, after all, supposed to be part of his creation. No, if you want to read about the real world you won't read about it in the Bible. You won't learn that the goldfish is member of the carp family by reading the Bible. *Genus Carassius* will remain a mystery to you.

JOHN: I suppose it will.

ERNEST: And that, if you don't mind me saying, is the big problem with the Bible.

JOHN: What, that it doesn't mention goldfish?

ERNEST: No, that it's just not relevant to the way we live our lives today. I want a book that tells me things I want to know about.

JOHN: Are we still talking about goldfish?

ERNEST: I believe you will find no mention of pandas in the scriptures. Nor even the kangaroo. Electricity doesn't get a look in. Neither does Japan. In fact, I dare say I could go on to mention many more things that the Bible fails to take account of. The planet Neptune for example.

JOHN: I'm sorry but I really don't understand your point.

ERNEST: My point is that people say the Bible contains answers. I have looked into the Bible many times in search of answers and I have never found them. When, for example, I wanted to find the answer to the question "What is the capital of Nicaragua?" I was completely let down by the Bible.

JOHN: Managua.

ERNEST: Pardon?

JOHN: The capital of Nicaragua is Managua.

ERNEST: Is it? Thank you. But you didn't learn that from the Bible, did you?

JOHN: No, from my geography teacher.

ERNEST: Time and time again I've looked in the Bible for answers and I haven't found them.

JOHN: Have you looked for answers that don't directly relate to goldfish?

ERNEST: Are you suggesting that the Bible *doesn't* have the answers to *all* life's questions? Because if you are then you are severely out of step with traditional church teachings.

JOHN: I don't know if the Bible has the answers to all life's questions but it does have the answers to some of the biggest ones. It tells us about how God loves us and how we can know him. It's full of poetry and parables, history and biographies, letters, laws, and proverbs.

ERNEST: But no fish.

JOHN: It's full of fish! Big fish, fish with coins in their mouths, fish in nets, fish served with bread al fresco, and even fishers of men.

ERNEST: But none of them gold in colour.

JOHN: It doesn't specify colour.

ERNEST: So some of them might actually be gold.

JOHN: Well . . . I suppose that might be so.

ERNEST: I may have to reassess my evaluation of the Bible. It may have more relevance than I had previously believed. It might even be able to help me with the answers I seek. Answers I have sought for years.

(John stands up to leave, he hands Ernest the Bible.)

JOHN: I have to leave now. Please keep this and read it. Perhaps it can help.

ERNEST: Thank you.

JOHN: Goodbye.

(Exit John. Ernest opens up the Bible.)

ERNEST: You never know. It might just be possible . . . Now where would I find the book of Jonah?

Links for the Interval
by Stephen Deal

Link to end Part One

These links can be used if you adopt the same format for the evening that we did and serve food and mark your quiz during the interval. Ad libbing is necessary for the link to begin Part Two. The appearance of Nova as M.C. helps to give continuity to the evening, but feel free to adapt or omit this material.

(At the end of the first part Nova enters.)

NOVA: Settle down. I know it's nearly break time but the bell hasn't gone yet. When the bell does go I want you all to *go to the dining hall and queue up for your food like civilised angels. (or *sit quietly like civilised angels while your food is served)*

Pardon, Watkins? No I don't know what's on the menu today. Fried manna I should imagine. Or maybe grilled manna. Or perhaps boiled manna – the possibilities are endless.

(A school bell rings.)

Don't move yet. The bell is for me, not for you.

Next lesson I shall be marking the quiz you should have completed by now. If, for some unimaginable reason, you have not yet finished it, I suggest you forgo your break and get it finished. There will be a whole aeon of detention for anyone who fails.

Right, off you go. Enjoy your break.

Link to begin Part Two

(Enter Nova.)

NOVA: Thank you, Michaels, you can stop throwing food at Stephenson.

Right, where were we? Oh yes. The quiz. Let's go on with marking that, shall we? I'll trust you to mark your own papers.

The answer to question number one is . . .

(Nova gives out the answers to the quiz.)

Right then, let's see who did well at this shall we? Who got more than X right? And who got more than X correct?

(When Nova has established who did best he awards a prize to the winners.)

The Rediscovery of the Bible
by Nick Page

CAST

NEWSREADER

KEVIN ETHICS

ARTHUR STREEBLY

ARCHBISHOP

ANGLER ONE

ANGLER TWO

News-type music, lights up on Newsreader *seated at desk, downstage right.*

NEWSREADER:	Good evening, this is the *News at Ten* on Monday the 20th of August 2154.
	It's been reported this morning that the twelve-year-old war in Indo-China is finally over. Unfortunately, a new one has started in Chino-India. That brings the total number of wars being fought in the world to 406. Not including Millwall away matches. Global Presidio Linford Christie III, when asked about the increasing violence and corruption in the world, stated that the breakdown was due to declining moral standards. He stated "There is nothing to guide us any more". Our Morality Correspondent Kevin Ethics reports.
	(Enter Kevin.*)*
KEVIN:	The decline in moral standards is not a new phenomenon. It was very much in evidence at the end of the twentieth century, but now, perhaps more than ever, people are feeling lost and without guidance. I asked historian Arthur Streebly if this is the worst it has ever been.
	(Enter Arthur.*)*
ARTHUR:	Yes, this loss of knowledge is only comparable to the aftermath of the Roman Empire.
KEVIN:	*(Knowledgeably.)* The Dim Ages.
ARTHUR:	Well, it's the Dark Ages actually.
KEVIN:	Right.
ARTHUR:	That was a time when many books, and other records were lost, and weren't rediscovered until the Renaissance.
KEVIN:	So are we entering another Dim Age?
ARTHUR:	Dark Age. Well, two disasters have contributed to the loss of knowledge. Firstly we had the dreadful Book Plague of the

mid-twenty-first century, when the mutant bookworm larvae destroyed 98% of all known paper-based records. Anything that had not been transferred to electronic media was lost. Secondly we had the ecological disaster of the Great Warming, which of course flooded so many areas and left churches, libraries, and much of the world under water.

(Exit Arthur.)

KEVIN: So, the question is, "In this new Dim Age, where can we look for guidance?" The traditional places, such as the church are still suffering from the effects of the Great Warming. With their historic places of worship destroyed they have been forced to base themselves in new areas. We spoke to the Archbishop of Chipping Sodbury.

(Enter Archbishop.)

ARCHBISHOP: In the olden days we used to have a thing called the Bible, but in the Warming and with all the flooding that followed, all our records were lost.

KEVIN: Don't you have any clue about what it contained?

ARCHBISHOP: Well it was all so long ago. Some fragments of it used to be read out in churches every Sunday – there was something called the Ten Commandments which told you how to live, and then there was the New Testament . . .

KEVIN: And were these important?

ARCHBISHOP: Well, some people thought they were. But when we looked through all the books stored on the Global Computer Library we found things like the Gardener's Bible and the Businessman's Bible, but not *the* Bible – the important one. We remember some of the rituals of course, and do those every Sunday.

KEVIN: Isn't that rather pointless?

ARCHBISHOP: Oh, no, the Church has always been rather good at endlessly repeating things without ever understanding why.

(Exit Archbishop.)

KEVIN: So there you have it. The world spirals downwards while the one thing which could provide a solution is apparently lost for ever. This is Kevin Ethics, *News at Ten*, Chipping Sodbury.

(Exit Kevin. Lights down on Newsreader.)

(Enter Anglers One and Two. They are in a boat and, rather unsurprisingly, they are fishing.)

ANGLER ONE: Look! Down there – a huge fish!

ANGLER TWO: Where? Oh, no, that's not a fish. It's the dome of St Paul's.

ANGLER ONE: You what?

ANGLER TWO: Saint Paul's – it was a church. Before the Warming, that is. There used to be a great city here – under all this water. Called London. Funny really, they built this thing called the Thames Barrier to protect themselves from a flood.

ANGLER ONE: Didn't work then?

ANGLER TWO: Well, against any normal flood maybe. Trouble was they hadn't oiled it properly. When the flooding came they just couldn't get it up in time.

ANGLER ONE: Hang on – I think I've got a bite . . .

ANGLER TWO: Reel it in then.

ANGLER ONE: It's fighting! I reckon it's a ten pounder at least!

(Fisherman One *reels in a Bible.*)

ANGLER ONE: Funny sort of fish.

ANGLER TWO: It's a book . . . The Holy Bib . . . *(Realises.)* Do you know what this is?

ANGLER ONE: Is it a trout?

ANGLER TWO: No, it's not a trout. It's something far more important than a trout!

ANGLER ONE: Salmon?

ANGLER TWO: Look, will you forget about fish! Does this look like a fish?

ANGLER ONE: It could be a very square shaped fish.

ANGLER TWO: It's not a fish. It's a Bible!

ANGLER ONE: You what?

ANGLER TWO: This isn't just any old book. They thought it was lost for ever and couldn't find it on their computers. This is *the* Bible. I saw it on the news last night. This is important!

ANGLER ONE: I see *(Pause.)* How do you cook it then?

(*Exit* Fishermen, *news-type music, lights up on* Newsreader.)

NEWSREADER: Good evening, this is the *News at Ten*, on the 21st of August 2154. The Bible has been rediscovered. Global Presidio Linford Christie III has ordered that it be broadcast world-wide just as soon as it's completely dried out. Kevin Ethics reports.

(*Enter* Kevin.)

KEVIN: The Bible was discovered by two anglers fishing over the remains of St Paul's. Experts at Watford University have freeze-dried it and are preparing to broadcast it to the waiting world. I spoke to Arthur Streebly, historian and Dim Age expert.

(*Enter* Arthur.)

ARTHUR:	Frankly, it's amazing. As far as we can tell, this is the most important day in the history of the Bible since the last time it was lost.
KEVIN:	In the Dim Ages.
ARTHUR:	*(Trying to keep his temper.)* No it wasn't in the *(Almost shouts.)* Dark Ages. We have discovered that it was lost in the early days of human history, and then rediscovered by accident during some building work. And, just like now, the ruler of that time ordered it to be broadcast to the people. *(Exit Arthur.)*
KEVIN:	But what difference will it make to the world around us? I spoke again to the Archbishop of Chipping Sodbury.
ARCHBISHOP:	Well. It's tremendous news. It will revitalise the church. It answers so many questions, you see – questions about God. If I may quote from the very first chapter "God created the heavens and the earth".
KEVIN:	Right. But what about the morality issue?
ARCHBISHOP:	Oh, it's an intensely practical book – it shows us the way to live our lives. If I may quote again "You must not steal. You must not murder". It's all so clear.
KEVIN:	How was it that so valuable a book was lost in the first place?
ARCHBISHOP:	Sadly, the truth is that people, many of them Christians, simply didn't realise what they had. One final quote, "Don't it always seem to go, that you don't know what you've got 'til it's gone."
KEVIN:	Is that from the Bible as well?
ARCHBISHOP:	No, it's from a Joni Mitchell song actually. *(Exit Archbishop.)*
KEVIN:	So there you have it. Is this a temporary light in our new Dim Age? Or is it a turning point for humanity? Only time will tell. This is Kevin Ethics, *News at Ten*, Chipping Sodbury. *(Exit Kevin, lights down on Newsreader.)*

Beginning with "J"

by Adrian Plass

CAST

CHLOE – The wife of Eutychus – a young woman

PRISCILLA – The mother of Eutychus – in her fifties

JASON – Eutychus' friend and workmate – a young man

DEMUS – Eutychus' friend – a young man

EUTYCHUS – A young man

This sketch is based on two Bible passages – JOHN 6.5–13 and ACTS 20.7–12. My proposed specific link between the two is, of course, highly speculative, but feasible enough, I think, to allow the drama to work well on a variety of levels. There is a lot of lightness and laughter to be developed, but there are also a number of moments that are potentially very moving for an audience. It seems to me essential that Priscilla is played by a strong and competent actress as her presence and dialogue are central supports for the piece. It may be thought necessary for the two Scripture passages to be read before the sketch begins, especially if the audience is unlikely to be familiar with the Bible. With audiences who do know the Bible well, it would probably be more effective not to read the passages.

The house of Eutychus and Chloe in Troas. Chloe is anxiously pacing the floor, but stops as she hears someone approaching.

PRISCILLA: *(Offstage.)* Is she in here? *(Enters.)*

CHLOE: Oh, Priscilla, I'm so glad you're here – I've been worried out of my mind.

PRISCILLA: Well, so that wretched girl of yours said, but she wouldn't say why. *(Holds her at arms' length and looks at her.)* Now you just calm yourself, sit down here, and tell me what's going on. No hurry – take your time.

CHLOE: It – it's Euty . . . *(She pronounces it "Yooty".)*

PRISCILLA: Eutychus? What's the matter with Eutychus? He's here, isn't he? The dawn's only just come up.

CHLOE: That's just it! He's *not* here.

PRISCILLA: Not here? Chloe, what do you mean?

CHLOE: The thing is – I don't know if Euty's told you about this job-splitting scheme he's just started with his friend Jason down at the marble works . . .

PRISCILLA: Oh, dear! Beware of Greeks sharing shifts. That's what my old mum used to say. Came to blows over divvying up the drachma, did they, Chloe, dear?

CHLOE: Oh, no, no, the job's going really well, it's just . . .

PRISCILLA: *(Coaxingly.)* Yes?

CHLOE: *(Builds to a crescendo.)* Well, the two of them were working together yesterday – some big order came up apparently, so everybody got called in – and afterwards they said they were going to try to drag Demus away from his market stall, and all go off to a – well, I'm not sure what it was, a sort of big religious meeting in the middle of the city, I think Euty said. A Jewish man called Paul talking about somebody else I can't remember whose name begins with a "J". Anyway, none of that's important. The point is that he hasn't been back all night, and there's no sign of any of the others and no news about anything from anyone and I'm really, really worried. I really am! Euty's never ever done anything like this before. Never! *(She starts to cry.)*

PRISCILLA: *(Holding and patting* Chloe.*)* Now, now, take it easy, I'm sure there's a very simple explanation if only we knew. After all, they're males, aren't they? The three of them probably came out of their meeting, wandered down the road, worked their way steadily through the menu at the nearest Macedonian take-away, drank far too much wine and ended up snoring like pigs in some doorway. They'll be back – and, if it's of any interest to you, he has done something like this before, but it was long before you knew him.

CHLOE: *(Momentarily distracted by surprise.)* He has?

PRISCILLA: *(Fondly reminiscing.)* Yes, he has. He was just a spindly lad at the time, and we were on our holidays down in Judea. I'll never forget it because of the truly amazing excuse he came up with afterwards. Talk about a fibber! *(Shakes her head and laughs.)* D'you want to hear about it?

CHLOE: *(Nods like a child.)* Mmmm.

PRISCILLA: What happened was – the little monkey insisted that he wanted to go out for a walk on his own, didn't he? Had to be on his own, or he wouldn't enjoy it, he said. Budding, blossoming independence, and all that. So his dad and I talked about it and agreed that as long as he didn't go too far and was back by the afternoon he could take a little lunch in a basket and go off by himself for an hour or so. And he went – proud as anything. Well, hours and hours later, with us worried out of our heads that some undiscerning lion had gobbled him up, independence and all, in strolls Master "I-can-look-after-myself-thank-you-very-much" Eutychus looking a bit tired but quite cheerful, pops his basket down on the table, and says he's sorry to have been so long, but he had to share his lunch with some people.

"Had to share your lunch with some people?" I said. "Yes," he said. "How many people?" I said. "Five thousand," he said. "Is that all?" I said. "Well, it might have been a few more than that," he said, "I didn't actually count them."

(They both laugh.) We were so glad to see him back safe and sound we hardly got cross at all, just told him there was no need to make silly excuses, and sent him off to bed. I sat with him for a while, and do you know what?

CHLOE: *(Totally absorbed by now.)* What?

PRISCILLA: Well, I asked him what *really* happened, quite gently – you know. Did he get lost or something and feel silly about telling us?

CHLOE: What did he say?

PRISCILLA: *(Thoughtful pause.)* Funny how you forget things, isn't it? I'm pretty sure he said he'd been at some kind of preaching thing just like this time, but the man doing the talking wasn't called Paul. Let me think . . . (pause) Do you know, I'm almost sure Eutychus said his name began with "J", like the one you said this Paul fellow was going to talk about last night. Now, is that a coincidence, or is that a coincidence?

CHLOE: *(Shaking her head.)* That's a coincidence.

PRISCILLA: Anyway, he stuck to his story – all excited inside, he was, I remember that – eyes shining. Told me with a dead straight face that this "J" character had borrowed his lunch, if you please – five little loaves and two small fish it was, and broken it up to feed these five thousand people who'd been so keen to hear what "J" had to say that they'd forgotten to take any food with them. He told me very solemnly that it took more than two hours for the man to break off enough bread and fish for everyone, and that's why he was late, because – wait for it – he knew I'd want the basket back. *(They both laugh again.)* He told it so well, he almost had me believing him.

CHLOE: But, what a funny story for Euty to make up.

PRISCILLA: *(Nods.)* Strange isn't the word. Gets it from his father, I think. I don't suppose the excuse he comes in with this morning will be half as interesting. *(Both laugh – Chloe shakes her head.)* But he definitely made up the lunch story. I mean, quite apart from the sheer absurdity of it all, when I went downstairs that night I remember peeping under the cloth inside the lunch basket where he'd left it on the table, and you'll never guess what I found.

CHLOE: *(Enthralled.)* What?

PRISCILLA: Five little loaves and two small fish. They hadn't even been touched.

(After a short reflective pause, Jason and Demus rush into the house looking dishevelled but very excited. Chloe and Priscilla jump to their feet.)

CHLOE: Jason! Demus! Where's Euty! What's happened? Why isn't he with you?

JASON: *(Throwing his arms wide and speaking as though he's announcing wonderful news.)* He's been killed!

(Chloe faints, all cluster noisily round to help. She slowly revives and is back on her feet before she speaks again.)

CHLOE: *(Fearfully.)* D–d–did you say Euty's been killed?

DEMUS: *(Enthusiastically.)* Yes, he fell out of a third floor window and broke his neck!

CHLOE: Oh, no!

PRISCILLA: *(Aghast, but in control.)* Would you two young men mind explaining why you insist on announcing my son's death as if it was a cause for celebration?

JASON: Because he's not dead! He's alive!

PRISCILLA: *(Pause, then rather hysterically.)* He's been killed but he's not dead? He had a fatal accident that resulted in him being alive? What on earth are you . . . *(Eutychus enters.)* Eutychus!

(Chloe faints again. All cluster round once more until she recovers and is seated.)

CHLOE: Oh, Euty, you're alive! They said you were dead.

MEN: *(All start speaking at once.)* He was! He stopped breathing! I broke my neck, etc.! etc.

PRISCILLA: *(Raises a hand to silence them.)* This beats the loaves and fishes into a cocked hat. Right, now, look, just tell us slowly and clearly what's been going on. Demus – you start.

DEMUS: Right, well, we went to hear Paul of Tarsus speak – all three of us, and it was up on the third floor of one of those tall buildings in the centre of town. The place was packed and hot, wasn't it, you chaps? *(Eutychus and Jason nod vigorously.)* Jason and I sat on the floor, and Eutychus perched right on the window ledge so that he'd . . . you know . . . get the benefit of the draught. And he fell asleep, didn't you, Eut?

EUTYCHUS: Yes, I . . .

JASON: We had our backs to him, you see, because we were listening to the speaker.

DEMUS: Great speaker – not flash or anything, but a great speaker.

PRISCILLA: *(Drily to her son.)* Hmmm, such a great speaker that he put you to sleep eh?

EUTYCHUS: Well, he *was* a very interesting speaker, mother, but, I dunno – maybe there's something about this new religion that makes people go on and on talking for hours and hours.

JASON: Anyway, neither of us realised that after three or four hours old Eut had just . . .

DEMUS: Dropped off.

JASON: Literally.

(Jason, Demus and Eutychus laugh uproariously but stop abruptly as they realise that Priscilla and Chloe are not amused.)

DEMUS: Yes, well, anyway, we suddenly heard this sort of dull thump down below and when we looked out we saw that Eut had . . . well, he'd fallen over backwards down on to the yard. We were devastated, weren't we Jason?

49

(Jason *nods earnestly.*) We rushed down as fast as we could, but when we got there . . . *(Shrugs.)* he was stone dead. Weren't you, Eut?

EUTYCHUS: So I'm told.

CHLOE: Oh Euty! Oh, my darling!

JASON: *(Seriously.)* I cried. You did too, didn't you, Demus? Howling like babies, we were. Horrible thing to happen – horrible! All blood and – oh, horrible! And – well, that was it really. That's what happened, isn't it, Demus?

DEMUS: Yep!

(Pause as Priscilla *and* Chloe *wait for more.)*

CHLOE: But – but – but – but – but –

PRISCILLA: *(With heavy sarcasm.)* I think Chloe is trying to say that you might have missed out one itsy-bitsy, teensy-weensy bit of the story. The trivial little detail about how he comes to be alive now when he was so recently deceased. Forgive our vulgar curiosity, but we'd love to know.

DEMUS: Oh, sorry! Of course – missed out the important bit. Well, I suppose Paul must have realised that no one was listening any more, so he stopped talking at last . . .

JASON: Great speaker, mind you.

DEMUS: Oh, yes, a terrific speaker – and he followed us downstairs and out to where the, er . . . Eutychus was lying. And then, well, he sort of looked at you and me, didn't he, Jason?

JASON: Yes, we were crying by then. And this Paul – he just kind of threw himself on the – on to Eutychus, and wrapped his arms round him as if . . . *(Searches for words.)*

DEMUS: As if he was dragging him back from somewhere . . .

(Pause.)

JASON: Then he got up – Paul I mean – and smiled at us, and said, "Don't worry, lads. Your friend's alive." And . . . he was.

DEMUS: We were a bit surprised.

JASON: Yeah, we were a bit. And then we thought, well, he's alive, not a scratch on him. Let's stay for the end of the meeting. So we did. And here we are now.

(Short silence.)

PRISCILLA: *(With a mother's sudden perception.)* You saw him again last night, didn't you, Eutychus? The man who borrowed your lunch all those years ago. You saw him, didn't you?

EUTYCHUS: *(Slowly, with a far-away look in his eyes.)* I don't remember anything about falling. I just remember finding myself going up this long tunnel, and he was standing at the end of it. He looked just the same. I walked right up to him and he smiled and said, "Shall I send you back, or will you come with me?" And I said, "Whatever you say, master." Then he put his arms round me, and suddenly I was – awake – alive – back to normal. But . . . I think normal's changed. *(He embraces* Chloe.*)*

PRISCILLA: *(Decisively.)* Jason – Demus – Eutychus, sit yourselves down. Right, you three, Chloe and I want to hear everything – and I mean everything – you know, about this man who's got a name beginning with "J".

(Fade to end.)

Two Women
by Les Padfield

CAST

MAN

WOMAN 1

WOMAN 2

MAN:	One day two women entered church to pray. The one, an upright and respected nun, with ease and grace approached, and on her knees began:
WOMAN 1	Oh, hello, God, I've no more than a few quick minutes to devote to you . . .
MAN:	The other, a young unmarried mother, rarely lifted up her eyes but barely sighed:
WOMAN 2:	O God, O God, without your love I'd never last – I seem to fail for ever.
WOMAN 1:	I know O God my faith is strong, I go each day to evensong, and always pray for you to bless and keep we chosen few.
WOMAN 2:	Forgive O Lord, the many times I live without a thought for you, and all the doubt I feel when you seem distant and unreal.
WOMAN 1:	Busy week. I've once again been asked to speak about my sterling work to curb the drought in all those lands (whose names I can't recall).
WOMAN 2:	Each day I stumble, fall, and go astray. I try to tell the truth and still I lie, and in your eyes I know my life is sin.
WOMAN 1:	I pray for three hours every other day.
WOMAN 2:	I know I shouldn't lose my temper so.
WOMAN 1:	And fast the very moment that I'm asked.
WOMAN 2:	And swear and curse when life seems so unfair.
WOMAN 1:	You could not wish for anyone so good.
WOMAN 2:	I'll turn again, O Lord, and try to learn.
WOMAN 1:	As some reward for this, let me become (I pray) Mother Superior one day!
WOMAN 2:	Teach me the way to follow you, and be my guide to hold me when I start to slide.
WOMAN 1:	Before I dash away, just one word more! Keep safe your valued servants from the waifs-and-strays that wander into church these days . . . Amen.
MAN:	And God in heaven, listening then, forgave the one, and gently reached to save and bless. But as the other needed less, He shed a tear, switched off, and went to bed.

Philip and the Ethiopian

by Nick Page

CAST

ONE

TWO

Enter One *and* Two. *They should perform this sketch with all the seriousness of "proper actors". In their minds they are recreating historical events with respect for history and uncanny accuracy.*

ONE	We present a tale from ancient times.
TWO:	From the world of the New Testament.
ONE:	I shall play Philip, an apostle, a man of God. A very holy man. Typecasting, I know, but there you go.
TWO:	*(Looking at script.)* And I shall play an Ethiopian . . . Hang on a minute. What does *that* word mean?
	(One whispers to Two.)
TWO:	*(Incredulous.)* No! Never! They didn't! *(Shocked.)* With a butter knife?
ONE:	It's true I'm afraid.
TWO:	Well, I'm not playing that for a start!
ONE:	You've got to. We are aiming for historical verisimilitude.
TWO:	It's all very well you aiming for historical vermilliontude, but you're not the one who has to play this Ethiopian Enoch.
ONE:	Eunuch.
TWO:	Whatever.
ONE:	Look, you can do it. Just think yourself into the character. You've got the range, the style, the natural ability to make us believe in this. You're going out there a nobody, and coming back a eunuch!
TWO:	*(Inspired.)* All right, all right, I'll give it a go.
ONE:	Good lad. *(To audience.)* We present the story of Philip and the Ethiopian Eunuch. Our story begins in Samaria, where Philip is visited by an angel.
	(One sits down on the stage, produces a loofah and mimes having a bath.)
TWO:	*(Fluttering around as an angel.)* Hail Philip.
ONE:	What are you doing in here?
TWO:	I'm an angel.
ONE:	Oh that's different. I thought you were the window cleaner. Only his day is Thursday.

TWO: I am come with a message. *(Gets out bit of paper.)* Blessed are you among women . . . oh, no that's an old one. Here we are – you're to get ready and go down to the desert road, from Gaza to Jerusalem.

ONE: But I've just had a bath. I don't want to get all dusty again.

TWO: I'm sorry, those are my instructions. Now, if you'll excuse me, I must go and get on with some heavenly praise and adulation.

*(*Two *flutters off. One *gets out of his bath.)*

ONE: So Philip did as he was told, and went and stood by the road. And he saw, coming towards him, an officer of Candace, the queen of the Ethiopians.

*(*Two *begins to "drive" around the stage, making the appropriate car noises.)*

ONE: And Philip was told by the Spirit to go and join the Ethiopian.

(He "runs" alongside Two.*)*

ONE: Excuse me.

TWO: *(Winding the window down.)* Do you mind? I'm trying to read. What are you doing out there, anyway? This is a dual carriageway. You should at least be displaying L-plates.

ONE: Hail, O Ethiopian eunuch.

TWO: There's no need to be personal. Anyway, I prefer the phrase "genitally challenged".

ONE: What's that book you're reading?

TWO: It's called the Old Testament. I can't understand it.

ONE: Two things, O not-quite-complete one, might be contributing to your lack of understanding. One – it needs to be expounded unto you.

TWO: And two?

ONE: You're holding it upside down. I tell you what, pull in your chariot at this lay-by and I'll expound.

*(*Two *applies the brakes, after giving appropriate hand signals.)*

TWO: I'm having a bit of a problem with the passage.

ONE: Your life is one medical challenge after another really, isn't it?

TWO: No – it's from Is-aye-eye-ay-aich.

ONE: Isaiah.

TWO: *(Looking upwards.)* It's from Is-aye-eye-ay-aich.

ONE: I suppose you think that's funny.

TWO: The particular passage is from Isaiah 53.

ONE: The truth, O high and mighty official, is that everyone needs the Bible explained to them. Let me hear the bit you're on about.

TWO: *(Reads.)* "He was like a sheep willing to be killed. *(Continues reading over* One's *next speech.)* He was quiet, as a lamb is quiet while its wool is being cut; he never opened his mouth. He was shamed and treated unfairly. He died without children to continue his family. His life on earth has ended."

ONE: *(Over preceding speech.)* And while the Ethiopian read the passage, Philip explained to him who the prophet was talking about, and it was as if the Bible came to life in the heart of the Ethiopian. And right there, he believed the good news about Jesus.

TWO: What do I have to do then?

ONE: Well, as my old Peter's always telling people, simply repent and be baptised.

(Two brings on a plastic bucket of water.)

TWO: *(Still in character.)* Look – here's water. Why don't I get baptised here?

ONE: *(Out of character.)* Is that it?

TWO: What's the matter now?

ONE: It's supposed to be an oasis. It's supposed to be a centre of lush vegetation in the midst of a desert.

TWO: Hold on.

(He fetches a small potted plant.)

TWO: Palm trees.

ONE: *(Making the best of it.)* Then both Philip and the officer went down into the water.

(They both attempt to get into the bucket. In the end they are reduced to putting in one foot each.)

ONE: And when Philip had baptised the officer, the Spirit of the Lord took Philip away. *(He attempts to get away from the bucket, but his foot is stuck.)* The Spirit of the Lord took Philip away . . . *(Finally he frees his foot and moves, rather balletically, away.)*

TWO: *(Turning as if to thank* Philip.) Thank you very much, that was a lovely service. Where did he go? *(He peers down into the bucket of water.)* Hello?

ONE: But the Ethiopian never saw him again.

TWO: Although we still exchange Christmas cards.

ONE: But throughout his life he remembered this encounter with the man who opened his eyes, and explained the Bible to him.

BOTH: The end.

(They exit.)

TWO: *(As he is leaving.)* Didn't heal me though, did he?

Link into the Five-minute Bible

by Stephen Deal

CAST

NOVA

DENNIS

Nova *enters followed by* Dennis.

DENNIS:	Sir! Sir!
NOVA:	Yes . . . er?
DENNIS:	Sir.
NOVA:	Yes, Dennis.
DENNIS:	I've found one, Sir.
NOVA:	Found what, boy?
DENNIS:	A book with everything in. It tells us about how the universe was created and how human beings fell from grace and how the earth was flooded and how there was a special people and how they were good and how they were bad and what happened when they were exiled and when they returned and . . .
NOVA:	Dennis . . .
DENNIS:	And then there are these songs and . . .
NOVA:	Dennis . . .
DENNIS:	And there were these men called prophets and . . .
NOVA:	Dennis . . .
DENNIS:	And . . .
NOVA:	Dennis, desist.
DENNIS:	Sorry, Sir.
NOVA:	I take it you have found a Bible.
DENNIS:	Yes, Sir.
NOVA:	And you wish to tell me all about it?
DENNIS:	Yes, Sir.
NOVA:	And how long will it take for you to tell me all about the Bible?
DENNIS:	Five minutes, Sir.
NOVA:	You can tell me all about the Bible in five minutes?
DENNIS:	No, no. I can't tell you all about the Bible in five minutes. But I can tell you what's in it.

NOVA: The entire contents of the Bible?

DENNIS: Yes, Sir.

NOVA: This should be interesting. Go ahead then and, if you can, I'll let you off doing that essay.

DENNIS: Five minutes then.

NOVA: Starting from . . . now.

(The "Five-minute Bible" sketch is performed.)

The Five-minute Bible
by Stephen Deal

CAST

> A
>
> B
>
> C
>
> D

This sketch is like no other. It must be delivered very fast from the start and get faster towards the end of the Old Testament section before a very brief pause leading into the New Testament section. The humour comes from the pace of delivery rather than the actual words. The four actors should rarely stop moving so the overall affect is a blur of words and action.

A: Ladies and gentlemen, we present to you . . .

B: The Bible . . .

C: In just five minutes.

D: Genesis.

A: In the beginning God created the heavens and the earth.

B: It took him just six days.

A: Which is pretty quick to build anything. Just ask the men who fitted my kitchen cupboards.

C: The pinnacle of his creation was humankind.

D: Specifically a man called Adam.

B: Who was quickly joined by a woman called Eve.

A: So far so good.

B: But . . . Eve was tempted by a serpent to eat from the tree of forbidden knowledge.

C: A serious mistake on her part. Which had a knock-on effect to Adam because sin had entered the world.

D: And shattered the relationship between people and God.

A: Adam and Eve had two sons called Cain and Abel.

   (B (Cain) kills D (Abel.)

C: As you can see the human race is off to a good start.

A: Where is your brother?

B: Am I my brother's keeper? Things went from bad to . . . Well . . . badder.

C: And God decided to wipe the slate clean and start again.

A: Noah. The planet's one good man. Was told to build an ark and rescue some livestock.

C: It rained and rained for 40 days and 40 nights.

B: Which had a detrimental effect on the environment.

C: So everybody and everything drowned. Except those aboard Noah's ark.

A: God promised he wouldn't destroy his creation again and as a sign of this covenant he gave us the . . .

B: Rainbow. Rushing on.

C: Because we're still only in Genesis.

A: The descendants of Noah built the tower of Babel, which was the Canary Wharf of its day. It brought about the division of nations.

B: Eventually Abraham came on the scene.

C: He became the father of the children of Israel. Soon came Jacob who wrestled with angels and dreamed of a ladder up to heaven.

B: He had many sons who became the tribes of Israel.

C: One of the sons was Joseph who went on to star in a hugely successful West End musical and who, strangely, had an Australian accent.

D: *(Sings.)* "I closed my eyes, drew back the curtains, and saw for certain, any dream will do".

A: No you didn't, we don't have time.

B: Joseph and his brothers ended up in Egypt.

C   But they out-stayed their welcome and eventually ended up as slaves.

D: Which brings us to the book of Exodus. How are we doing for time?

A: Badly. We'll have to speed up. Ready?

BCD: *(Together.)* Ready.

A: Moses met God in the desert.

B: He was disguised as a burning bush.

A: God that is, not Moses.

D: God told Moses to free his people from slavery.

C: Moses went to see Pharaoh who laughed in his face.

A: So Moses and God came up with a plan.

B: God visited upon Egypt a series of plagues, culminating in the death of the first-born children.

C: After which Pharaoh was only too pleased to see the back of Moses and the children of Israel.

D: So off they set, into the wilderness.

A: But before they could get very far Pharaoh changed his mind and sent his army to bring them back.

B: Moses found himself trapped between the Red Sea and a fearsome army.

D: What could he do?

A: Stand and fight?

B: Or run and drown?

C: A tricky choice. Fortunately there was a third option.

B: Run and not drown.

A: Yes folks, God through Moses parted the Red Sea and the children of Israel escaped.

C: While the Egyptian army was washed away like a stain in a Daz Ultra commercial.

B: The children of Israel wandered for 40 years around the wilderness. They were given the Ten Commandments and they finally made it into the promised land.

A: Except Moses who died before reaching it.

C: Now the books of Leviticus, Numbers and Deuteronomy.

B: Lots of laws.

A: And some battles.

C: Then the book of Joshua.

ABD: *(Sing.)* "Joshua fought the battle of Jericho, Jericho. Joshua fought the battle of Jericho, and the walls came tumbling down."

C: And on to Judges.

A: A book that paints pictures of its heroes, warts and all. Deborah, a gifted lady.

B: Barak, unwilling to take on responsibility.

C Gideon, started out as a coward, became a remarkable military strategist, and then tailed off as an idol worshipper.

A: Jephtah, a brave soldier who didn't always think before he opened his big mouth.

B: *(As Jephtah.)* Lord, if you help me win this battle I will sacrifice to you as a burnt offering whatever comes out of my door when I get home.

D: Nice thought, Jeph, but haven't you forgotten that you live with your only daughter?

B: *(As Jephtah.)* Oops!

C: And of course there was good old Samson and the most expensive haircut in history.

A: Which brings us to the end of Judges and on to Ruth.

B: A book about love and loyalty against a background of violence and racism.

A: Then on to 1 Samuel and 2 Samuel. Which might better be called the Book of David. Saul was Israel's first king but David was her greatest.

A: In his youth David fought the mighty Goliath.

(There is a very quick enactment of the David and Goliath battle.)

C: Then David spent some time as an outlaw. But when Saul died David succeeded him.

B: He fought many battles and had an affair with Bathsheba.

A: He also had a major problem with one of his sons, Absalom.

D All in all, a fairly typical royal family saga.

C: Now on to 1 and 2 Kings.

B: The golden age of Israel. The reign of King Solomon.

A: Solomon was very wise because he nearly chopped a baby in half.

C: Solomon was a great king because he built the great temple.

D: Solomon had a great sex life. He had seven hundred wives and three hundred concubines.

B: But his wives led him astray and he started to build temples for false gods.

A: So after his death the country fell apart and eventually was invaded by the Babylonians.

C: The temple was destroyed. And the children of Israel were taken into exile.

D: The books of 1 and 2 Chronicles cover the same ground and . . .

A: Ezra, and Esther cover the period in exile in Babylon and the return of the people to Israel . . .

B: And the rebuilding of the temple.

C: Interestingly, Esther is the only book in the Bible not actually to mention God. Now come the Wisdom books.

A: Job, a story of steadfast faith in the face of great suffering.

B: Psalms, 150 hymns, prayers and poems covering the full range of human emotion.

C: Proverbs, lots of wisdom

D: Ecclesiastes, lots more wisdom.

A: Song of Songs, lots of sex.

B: Then come the books of the prophets. The general theme of which is, turn back to the Lord O Israel.

C: Isaiah and Jeremiah.

A: Lamentations, author unknown, very sad. Ezekiel.

C: Daniel, famed for his exploits with lions.

B: Then Hosea, Joel, Amos and Obadiah.

A: Jonah, swallowed by a great fish, thrown up on a beach and going to Ninevah.

BC: Micah, Nahum, Habakkuk, Zephaniah, Haggai.

D: Zechariah and Malachi.

A: Which brings us, exhausted, to the end of the Old Testament.

(All four actors pause briefly and recover their breaths.)

B: The New Testament.

ACD: Right.

B: The New Testament starts with the Gospels.

A: Meaning the good news.

C: Matthew, Mark, Luke and John.

D: The books about Jesus.

B: Jesus was born of the virgin Mary, in a stable in Bethlehem.

C: He was baptised by his cousin, John the Baptist.

A: Then he spent three years teaching and healing throughout the land.

B: During this time he . . .

C: Turned water into wine. Walked on water.

A: Fed over five thousand people with just two loaves and five fish.

C: Raised Lazarus from the dead.

D: Healed the sick.

B: Told many stories.

C: Upset the Pharisees.

A: Upset the money lenders.

B: But he never sinned.

C: He never turned his back on anyone.

D: And he never deserved to die.

A: A plot was hatched against him.

D: He broke the bread and he poured out the wine.

B: A friend . . .

C: Judas . . .

B: Betrayed him.

C: He was taken before Pilate and tried.

A: And although he was innocent he was found guilty and sentenced to die.

B: Crucified.

D: On a hill outside the city.

 (One of the actors strikes a crucifixion pose. This is held for a few seconds.)

C: They buried him in a tomb sealed with a large rock.

A: But on the third day he rose from the dead.

B: And was seen by many people.

C: He told his friend Peter to feed his lambs.

D: The Acts of the Apostles.

A: Jesus ascends to heaven.

C: The Holy Spirit descends like tongues of fire.

B: And the Church is born.

D: Stephen is stoned to death. The first Christian martyr.

A: Saul sees a blinding light on the road to Damascus.

B: He changes his name to Paul and becomes a great Christian missionary.

C Paul and others write many letters of encouragement and teaching.

D: Romans.

A: Corinthians 1 and 2, Galatians, Ephesians.

B: Philippians, Thessalonians 1 and 2.

C: One Timothy, 2 Timothy, Titus and .

D: Hebrews, James.

B: Peter, Peter, John, John, John.

C: Jude.

D: But the final book of the Bible is not a letter but rather a vision.

A: The end of this world and the beginning of a new world.

B: Of Jesus come in glory.

C: The Revelation of Saint John the Divine.

D: The Bible ends thus.

A: He who testifies to these things says . . .

C: Yes, I am coming soon.

D: Amen.

B: Come Lord Jesus.

A: The grace of the Lord Jesus be with God's people

ALL: Amen.

Sketches on Open Book Themes

The Greatest Story Ever Sold

by Stephen Deal

The Bible is a book about people whose experiences of life may be more similar to our own than we think. This is the idea introduced by this sketch which can be staged as simply or elaborately as your production allows. A table with a few Bibles stacked on it will serve as well as an authentic book shop set complete with working till. Although the script calls for a female shop assistant and a male customer, minor judicious editing should allow for some flexibility when it comes to casting. What is important is that the actors spark off each other and keep the piece flowing along. Hand props should be kept to hand. Pam shouldn't need to go and look for the Bible; it should just be there. The passing of the book back and forth can be used for comedic affect.

CAST

PAM

CUSTOMER

Pam *is serving at the counter of The Good Book Shop.* Customer *approaches.*

PAM: Hello, welcome to The Good Book Shop. How may I help you?

CUSTOMER: I'd like to buy a good book please.

PAM: Certainly sir. Here you are.

  (She hands Customer *a Bible.)*

CUSTOMER: I'm sorry but this appears to be a copy of the Bible.

PAM: Yes sir.

CUSTOMER: But I want *a* good book, not *the* Good Book.

PAM: Yes sir.

CUSTOMER: I'm sure the Good Book is a good book but it's not what I'm looking for.

  (He hands the Bible back to Pam.*)*

PAM: Are you sure?

CUSTOMER: Yes. I want a block-busting roller-coaster of a literary ride.

PAM: A story that spans generations?

CUSTOMER: Yes. An epic that confronts the human condition.

PAM: A tale of love and betrayal?

CUSTOMER: Yes.

PAM: Here you are then.

  (She gives him back the Bible.)

CUSTOMER: But I don't want to read the Bible. I want a book that's relevant to me, here and now, on the brink of a new millennium. I want a book about real people, not perfect, God-fearing holy-rollers.

PAM: That's a relief.

CUSTOMER: Why?

PAM: Because, with one exception, you've as much chance of stumbling over a perfect, God-fearing person in the Bible as you have of finding a vegetarian crocodile.

CUSTOMER: Oh nonsense, who was that guy with the tablets?

PAM A pharmacist?

CUSTOMER: Moses. The Ten Commandments and all that. What about him?

PAM: Oh yes, he was a great man of God.

CUSTOMER: Well, there you are then.

PAM: And he murdered someone.

CUSTOMER: Did he?

PAM An Egyptian.

CUSTOMER: All right, perhaps not the best example. What about Noah? He's the kind of man the Bible's all about. He was holy and kind to animals.

PAM: He was fond of the odd drink too.

CUSTOMER: The occasional tipple maybe.

PAM: If that's all it takes to make you fall unconscious naked in a tent next door to your children, then I'm sure he hardly touched a drop.

CUSTOMER: You are missing my point. I want to read about people I have something in common with.

PAM: What do you do for a living?

CUSTOMER: You're hoping I'm going to say fisherman or shepherd or something like that so you can tell me the Bible is full of people like me. Well, hard luck, I work as an insurance claims assessor.

PAM: *(Quoting.)* Acts 19.19: "A number who had practised sorcery brought their scrolls together and burned them publicly."

CUSTOMER: So what?

PAM: *(Triumphantly.)* When they calculated the value of the scrolls, the total came to fifty thousand drachmas.

CUSTOMER: Oh very clever. But supposing my wife wants to borrow the book when I've finished? She likes family sagas with twists and turns and strong female characters to identify with.

PAM: The Book of Ruth. Barbara Taylor Bradford eat your heart out.

CUSTOMER: Yes, but I want something a bit more . . . You know . . .

PAM: No.

CUSTOMER: Well, raunchy I suppose.

PAM: Song of Songs. You'll never look at a bunch of grapes in the same way again.

CUSTOMER: Now listen, I do not want to buy a copy of the Bible. I just want a book I can read and enjoy.

PAM: A best-seller?

CUSTOMER: Yes.

PAM: Then you want the Bible.

CUSTOMER: No, no, no.

PAM: I'm sorry sir, but I don't understand. You say you want a book that reflects your own situation and tells stories about people you can relate to, but you're not prepared to read the Bible.

CUSTOMER: OK, OK, you win. Please may I have a copy of the Bible.

PAM: Certainly sir. *(She hands* Customer *a copy of the Bible.)* Now you will look after it, won't you?

CUSTOMER: Of course.

PAM: You won't neglect it?

CUSTOMER: It's just a book. A great book maybe, but just a book.

PAM: And you will make sure it gets plenty of exercise. You won't leave it to just moulder on a bookshelf.

CUSTOMER: I thought I was buying a book not a puppy.

PAM: And I thought you understood. The Bible is the living Word of God. It's alive and potentially dangerous.

CUSTOMER: Dangerous?

PAM: Hebrews 4.12: "For the word of God is living and active. Sharper than any double-edged sword."

CUSTOMER: Are you sure it's safe to own?

PAM: Have you seen those big black leather covers on many Bibles?

CUSTOMER: Yes.

PAM: Most people think they're there to protect the Bible.

Rewards of Office
by Stephen Deal

This is the second sketch which raises the idea of seeing parallels between our own experiences and those of people in the Bible story. All the characters should be on stage from the start of this piece. Ideally the biblical characters would remain unlit until they are called upon to appear and would fade into darkness when they have finished participating. (A simple alternative would be to have them standing with their backs to the audience until it is time for them to turn around and speak.) It is entirely up to you whether you dress the biblical characters in authentic costume to contrast with Jeremy's *modern dress. An alternative might be to dress them all in black and give them simple props to help identify them. For example,* Moses *might carry stone tablets,* Gideon *a fleece, and* Ehud *a sword.*

CAST

JEREMY

GIDEON

MOSES

EHUD

(Jeremy sits at his desk, using the phone. He is obviously stressed. Behind him, unseen by Jeremy, *stands* Gideon, Moses *and* Ehud.)

JEREMY: *(Into the telephone and with forced cheerfulness.)* Hello Clive? Clive me old mucker, me old mate, how are you? . . . Good, good. And how's Sarah? . . . Susan, I meant Susan, of course . . . You're divorced? Oh I am sorry. When did that happen? Five years ago? Look Clive, I know it's an awful cheek but I wonder if you could let me do you a favour? . . . It's Jeremy. Remember we met in Tenerife . . . Yes it must have been eight or nine years ago now . . . Time flies. Anyway, you said if I ever needed a favour to give you a call . . . In the bar, remember? . . . Yes we had had a lot to drink. You mentioned at the time that you were in galvanised widgets. Well you're not going to believe this but my company is producing splange sprockets for the galvanised widget and I'm in a position to do you fabulous deal . . . Clive? Clive, are you there? Clive?

(He taps the phone desperately.)

(To himself.) Keep calm Jeremy, keep calm. It's not a matter of life or death. It's only your job that's on the line. Maybe if I try Mike Hutchings over at Allied Splange . . . I'm sure he won't mind if I call him at the hospital . . . The by-pass operation was hours ago now. Now where's his number?

(Moses steps forward.)

MOSES: Can I help?

JEREMY: *(Very surprised.)* Who the blazes are you?

MOSES: I am Moses of the house of Levi.

JEREMY:	I don't want to buy any jeans.
MOSES:	No, Moses who led the Children of Israel out of Egypt.
JEREMY:	The guy in the Old Testament?
MOSES:	Yes.
JEREMY:	Am I having a nervous breakdown?
MOSES:	Yes.
JEREMY:	Oh.
MOSES:	Do you remember St Peter's?
JEREMY:	If you're telling me the Pearly Gates are swinging wide open for me – you'll have to wait while I make one last call.
MOSES:	No, St Peter's church. You used to go there with your parents when you were a child.
JEREMY:	On the High Street, next to the cinema.
MOSES:	It's a carpet warehouse now.
JEREMY:	St Peter's?
MOSES:	No the cinema. St Peter's church is fine.
JEREMY:	We used to learn all about you. Didn't you do that trick with the Red Sea?
MOSES:	Yes.
JEREMY:	And the Ten Commandments, they were yours weren't they?
MOSES:	I was just the messenger.
JEREMY:	It's funny how it all comes back to me. I haven't thought of you in years.
MOSES:	I'm part of your heritage.
JEREMY:	That's good, I haven't got much of a future. Look I love to chat but I really must make this call.
	(He picks up the phone.) I've really blown it this time. I made a huge mistake on an account and got involved in something a little bit dodgy. Now I'm about to lose everything . . . Why am I telling you? You were great at what you did.
MOSES:	I made mistakes. Big ones.
JEREMY:	Did you ever misplace an order of splange sprockets and endanger your job? We're talking major error here. No one will touch me after this.
MOSES:	I killed someone.
JEREMY:	*(He puts the phone down again.)* Well yes I can see how you would consider that a big mistake. It must have been a shame to ruin your life after you'd been so successful with all that stuff about plagues and pharaohs and wildernesses. Fancy leading a people out of bondage and then blowing it big time.

MOSES: It happened before all that occurred.

JEREMY: Are you saying that the big guy, God, used you even after you did such a terrible thing?

MOSES: Yes.

JEREMY: Ah, but then you couldn't have had enemies like I've got. Those guys in accounts and data transfer hate my guts. Even if by some miracle I do get a second chance those guys are out to get me. They're just watching for me to mess up.

(Gideon *steps forward.*)

GIDEON: Then you need to hide what you're doing. Use subterfuge and strategy.

JEREMY: And you would be?

GIDEON: Gideon.

JEREMY: The Bibles in hotels man?

GIDEON: I believe my name is linked to such a project, yes.

JEREMY: And didn't you have a Golden Fleece?

GIDEON: That was an entirely different person. My fleece was wet and then dry.

JEREMY: That's right. And you were the guy with the huge army that God would only allow you to use a fraction of. I'm amazed I can remember all this.

GIDEON: Stories have power.

JEREMY: What were you saying about subterfuge? I like the sound of that.

GIDEON: When I was living with my father we had many enemies. The Midianites were continually raiding our land. Times were desperate and we had little food. If we tried to thresh wheat to make bread out in the open the Midianites would see the clouds of chaff from miles away and would know exactly where we were.

JEREMY: What did you do?

GIDEON: We had a wine press. It was a large hole in the ground and it had a lid. I threshed the wheat in there. It was hot, hard work. It was nowhere near as easy as doing it out in the open but at least it gave us a chance to make enough to survive until the time was right to deal with the situation. In fact that was what I was doing when the angel of the Lord came to visit me.

JEREMY: So you suggest that I keep my head down until the time is right to make a move?

GIDEON: It's a thought.

JEREMY: There's just one problem.

GIDEON: Only one. You are fortunate indeed.

JEREMY: The managing director of this company is a crook. He knows precisely what's been going on. I've been asked by the people in my department to speak to him but it won't do any good. All that man wants is people to grovel to him.

(Ehud *steps forward.*)

EHUD: Then you must take radical action. Slay him.

JEREMY: It's a nice thought but a little extreme even for these circumstances. And who are you?

EHUD: I am Ehud son of Gera.

JEREMY: Who?

EHUD: Ehud.

JEREMY: I'm sorry but I've never heard of you.

EHUD: My story is told in the book of Judges, chapter 3.

JEREMY: You'll have to remind me.

EHUD: My people were being oppressed by Eglon the king of Moab. I was sent to deliver them from him.

JEREMY: And so you killed him?

EHUD: It was the way things were done in those days.

JEREMY: How did you get close enough? Our MD is always surrounded by advisers and toadies.

EHUD: I told him I had a secret to tell him. He sent everyone away.

JEREMY: And then what?

EHUD: He was a very fat man. I took my sword, which was about 18 inches long, in my left hand and I drove it into his belly. It went in so deep it came out of the back as the rolls of fat closed over the wound at the front.

JEREMY: Yuk. That's horrible. I didn't know that the Bible had stories like that in it.

EHUD: Well it does. After I'd done the deed I left the throne room and locked the door from the outside and fled.

JEREMY: Weren't King Eglon's advisers suspicious when they found the door locked?

EHUD: They thought the king had gone to relieve himself so they waited and waited. It gave me time to escape.

JEREMY: So you got away because they were too embarrassed to disturb the king because they thought he was on the toilet?

EHUD: Yes. My point is that I had to resort to extreme measures to bring about the right result.

JEREMY: I'll say. But however tempting it is I can't stick a sword into our MD.

EHUD: Ah but perhaps a metaphorical one? You have to do the right thing. And you can use perceived weakness against your foe. I was left handed and that was considered a disability in my day. Your managing director probably thinks you are too scared to act against him.

JEREMY: I could bring the whole company crashing down on me.

EHUD: Samson did that. The Lord gave him the strength.

JEREMY: He's not here as well is he?

EHUD: No, it's Wednesday. He's having his hair done.

JEREMY: Oh well, here goes . . . (Jeremy *picks the phone up and dials.*) Hello, Sandra? It Jeremy from Sales. Is Sir Gerald in? I need to talk to him . . . He's what? He's indisposed? Oh I see. He's been ever such a long time but you're too embarrassed to disturb him . . . Well give him a few more minutes and then I'd call a doctor.

A Sign of Hope
by Nick Page

This sketch focuses on disappointment and the birth of Jesus as a source of hope. It is set in a school reunion, at Christmas. Four old friends meet up again after many years to find out that their life is not, perhaps, all that they'd hoped it would be.

The sketch should be played at a very relaxed pace. It is a gentle piece, a picture of people's lives. The air should not be one of doom and gloom, but it should be reflective, even a little melancholy at times.

CAST

GEORGE – A middle manager. Dressed in a casual suit and tie. Pretty straight looking. Glasses.

SUSAN – A mother. She has dressed up for the evening, but is pretty conventional.

JOHNNY – A car salesman. He has a flashy suit and tie on. He is loud and confident.

JANICE – An environmental campaigner. She wears big, baggy combat trousers and a huge woolly jumper that has seen better days. Her hair is dyed blue.

There is a table centre stage, around which they will sit. They have drinks and on the table is a plate of crisps, etc. Enter George and Susan. They are carrying drinks.

GEORGE: Why did we come?

SUSAN: What do you mean? It will be nice to see the old crew again.

GEORGE: "Nice." This is obviously some new definition of the word that I wasn't previously aware of.

SUSAN: Look, George. I know that things are difficult for us at the moment.

GEORGE: Us? Difficult for us? Difficult for me, you mean.

SUSAN: It's not just you, is it? There are more of us in this family.

GEORGE: *(Pause.)* Yes. I know. I'm sorry. I'm letting it get to me.

SUSAN: It's all right. Come on. Let's sit down.

            (They sit at a table.)

GEORGE: *(Looking around.)* There are a few faces I recognise here. Can't recall the names.

SUSAN: *(Pointing.)* Oh look! There's old Phillpott!

GEORGE: Where? Good Lord. He hasn't changed a bit . . .

            (They look at each other.)

GEORGE: Well, apart from losing his hair. And the zimmer frame. And that peculiar shaking movement. He's the same old headmaster I remember.

(Enter Johnny.)

JOHNNY: Who do I see here?

GEORGE: *(Rising to greet him.)* Johnny!

JOHNNY: You're looking great!

GEORGE: You look just the same. It's incredible!

SUSAN: Hello Johnny.

JOHNNY: Susan! *(She shakes his hand.)* What's this? What about a kiss?

(She kisses him. Apparently reluctantly.)

JOHNNY: It's great to see you both. How are you doing?

GEORGE: Good, good.

JOHNNY: Both still together after all these years. Who'd have thought it?

SUSAN: What about you. Is your wife here?

JOHNNY: Er . . . no. No. She couldn't come. One of her heads. *(Sitting down.)* Anyway, what are you doing with yourself?

GEORGE: I'm in contract cleaning.

JOHNNY: You're a cleaner?

GEORGE: I *manage* a load of cleaners.

JOHNNY: Just winding you up. I always knew you'd "clean up". Clean up. Get it?

SUSAN: I take it you're not a comedian.

JOHNNY: Eh? No, no, no. Sarukis. *(Pronounced sar-oo-kees.)*

SUSAN: Isn't that a kind of fish?

JOHNNY: Cars. Japanese. Got an import business. These are dream machines, 16 valve, 3 litre. Quiet as a mouse, built like tanks. Can't keep up with demand.

(To Susan.) What about you, Susan?

SUSAN: Children. You know. Little noisy things. Built like tanks. Can't keep up with their demands.

JOHNNY: How many?

SUSAN: Two. And you?

JOHNNY: Yeah, one. Little girl – Rose. By my first marriage. Here's her picture. *(He takes a photo from his wallet.)* Little Rosie.

SUSAN: Oh, she's sweet!

JOHNNY: Just turned three. She and her mother live up north somewhere. I'd like to see her more often, but you know how it is. *(He puts the photo back in his wallet.)*

(Enter Janice.)

JANICE: Hello.

SUSAN: Janice!

GEORGE: Jan! How great to see you. You're looking . . . you're looking . . . blimey. What is that in your hair?

JANICE: It's woad.

SUSAN: Woad?

JANICE: The ancient druids wore it. It's a protection. It wards off evil forces.

GEORGE: Not to mention flies.

JOHNNY: Have a drink?

JANICE: No thanks. I've got some water.

JOHNNY: Is that all?

JANICE: *(Seriously.)* It is pure. I value purity.

GEORGE: So let me guess. You're a nuclear scientist.

JANICE: Very funny. I'm a protester, actually. I'm camping out on the common. You know, where they want to build the ring road.

JOHNNY: Don't I know it. Boy we really need that road. It will take loads of pressure off the city centre . . .

(He catches sight of Janice's expression.)

JOHNNY: Well, it's just my opinion.

JANICE: Do you know what this obsession with the car is doing to the environment? Don't you care about that? Don't you care about the pollution they cause? Cars are a typical example of the greedy way we abuse this planet.

JOHNNY: Right.

JANICE: Anyway, what do you do?

(He is about to answer and then he changes his mind.)

JOHNNY: Oh you know, this and that . . .

SUSAN: *(To Janice, rescuing him.)* Are you married . . .

JANICE: I have a partner, if that's what you mean.

SUSAN: Is he here?

JANICE: No. He couldn't come. He's underground at the moment. Tunnelling.

JOHNNY: I bet he's really boring. *(Laughs, then catches sight of* Janice's *face.)* "Boring", right? Joke?

JANICE: You're a car salesman aren't you?

JOHNNY: Who told you?

JANICE: It just came to me.

JOHNNY: Well yes I am. And proud of it. I sell good cars. Cars that people want to buy.

JANICE: Cars that are killing the planet.

JOHNNY: *(Annoyed.)* Look, I've worked hard for my business. I've built it up from scratch and I don't need you lecturing me. Nobody can take it away from me. Not you, not the bank manager, not the divorce lawyer. Nobody!

            (Pause.)

GEORGE: "Divorce lawyer?"

JOHNNY: Ah. Sorry about that. Bit stressed there. Well, there you have it. Marriage number two has gone the same way as marriage number one. Only quicker. It didn't quite work out the way I'd hoped. She left me.

SUSAN: I'm sorry.

JOHNNY: So am I. You know I really hoped this one would work. She was great, Susie. She was going to make me happy. She was going to be someone to stay with me for life. Instead all I've got is this lousy car business.

GEORGE: I thought you said it was doing OK.

JOHNNY: It is. It's doing great. I'm flipping rich. It's still lousy though.

            (Pause.)

GEORGE: Well, if it makes you feel any better, things aren't great in our household.

JOHNNY: You mean you two . . .

GEORGE: Oh no, nothing like that. I've been made redundant.

JOHNNY: What? But you said . . .

GEORGE: I know. it wasn't exactly the truth. I was "downsized".

JOHNNY: Oh mate. I don't know what to say.

GEORGE: There's nothing to say. It's pretty hopeless. I'm middle-aged. Washed up. The management consultant they brought in said I was surplus to requirements. I'd have liked to downsize him. With an axe.

SUSAN: Don't worry darling. You'll find something.

JOHNNY: Yeah. Keep your spirits up.

GEORGE:	I can't see me getting another job in this climate. I'll just have to make the most of it.
JANICE:	I hate that kind of talk. "Make the most of it!" You've got to fight. That's what I'm doing. I mean, it would be no good if we sat down and said, well the earth is dying, let's just make the most of it.
SUSAN:	Is that what you think is happening?
JANICE:	I know it. Every year more trees die. Acid rain and pollution are destroying the lakes. Lead poisons the air. The earth is dying.
SUSAN:	So what's the point? If all you're saying is true, why do we go on? I mean, look at George – worn out and thrown away. Johnny's lonely and you think the world is going to end. What happened to us all? We had such high hopes when we were here. We were going to change the world.
GEORGE:	We should have known better.
SUSAN:	No. There must be hope. There has to be. You know, when I had our first boy, I held him in my arms and just looked at him. It seemed like hours. And I thought then that there is always hope. That's what a child is. A sign of hope in a dark world.
JOHNNY:	Yeah, you're right. Come on, a toast. *(He holds up his glass.)* To us.
OTHERS:	To us.
JANICE:	Happy Christmas everyone.
ALL:	Happy Christmas.
	(They raise their glasses and drink. There is a pause. Then blackout and exit.)

Forgive Us Our Trespasses

by Nick Page

This sketch follows on from "A Sign of Hope". It is a sketch about the longing for forgiveness and a new start. The time is later the same evening. The four school friends are more relaxed, more genial. The sketch should be played at the same gentle pace and the ending should be poignant rather than tragic.

It is a reflective look at the damage people do to their lives and their desire to somehow put things right; the desire that we all have to be loved and made whole.

Dress: as before. The lads have taken their jackets off and loosened their ties.

CAST

GEORGE

SUSAN

JANICE

JOHNNY

School reunion as before. George, Susan, Janice *and* Johnny *are sitting around the table.*

GEORGE: *(Finishing an anecdote.)* And then that time we diverted the traffic through the school drive!

JANICE: Yeah. I remember! The things that flood back at a school reunion.

GEORGE: My Dad kept me grounded for a week.

JOHNNY: I remember your old man. Boy, he could be tough. How is he?

GEORGE: He died three years ago.

JANICE: I'm sorry.

GEORGE: It's OK. You know, nothing I could do would ever satisfy him. You remember when I had long hair? I knew he hated long hair. And I was at university, and he was coming to visit me, and I knew we were going to have a confrontation.

JOHNNY: What happened?

GEORGE: I chickened out. I had it cut. He got out of the car and the first words he said were, "Your hair's too short." I don't know what it was, but we could never talk to each other. Not really talk. It was like there was a wall between us. The best we could do was lob messages over the top. I wish I could have said to him the things I really wanted to say.

JANICE: Why didn't you?

GEORGE: Don't be stupid, I'm English. I wanted to tell him things. I wanted . . . Oh I don't know. I wanted us to forgive each other. *(Uncomfortable pause.)*

JOHNNY: Still, they were great times, weren't they? Best days of your life.

SUSAN: I wouldn't go that far. I mean, you know, being teenagers. Growing up. There was a fair bit of pain as well.

JOHNNY: Yeah, but that's just par for the course isn't it? I mean you can't make an omelette without breaking eggs, can you, Jan?

JANICE: I wouldn't know. I don't eat baby chicks.

JOHNNY: Well it's true. Stuff happens. You've got to deal with it.

SUSAN: Ah, there speaks the good old Johnny. How the years roll back.

JOHNNY: What's that supposed to mean?

SUSAN: "Look after number one." That was what you used to say, wasn't it?

JOHNNY: I was young.

GEORGE: Not that young.

JOHNNY: All right, so I wasn't a saint.

SUSAN: Johnny, you were horrible.

JOHNNY: *(Pause.)* No, don't beat about the bush, tell me what you really think.

SUSAN: Well you were.

JOHNNY: You've never forgiven me, have you? You've never forgotten.

SUSAN: If you mean the way that you dumped me, no I haven't forgotten. I spent years trying to get over you.

JOHNNY: I can understand that. I was pretty hot stuff.

SUSAN: Johnny. I was fifteen. The fact I was devastated does not mean that I want to change things. Personally I rank you as something best forgotten. You are filed away in the "Do Not Repeat" drawer, along with the Bay City Rollers and tank tops. One of my more spectacular mistakes.

JOHNNY: *(Sarcastically.)* Cheers.

SUSAN: *(More gently.)* Like you said, we were young. It's just sometimes the mistakes leave scars. And despite it all, despite whatever happiness comes along, you can still look at the scar and remember how you got it, and who inflicted the wound.

JOHNNY: Well I'm sorry. No, really I am. I mean, come on, you know what I was like. I was the centre of the universe. Nothing else mattered. The trouble is, I don't think I've ever really grown out of it. I'm sorry.

SUSAN: It's alright. Really.

JOHNNY: And anyway – look at you, mother of two, happily married. And look at me. Still self-obsessed, and still on my own.

SUSAN: Maybe you and your wife can get together again.

JOHNNY: No. I don't think so. You know what happens. When things aren't good, you say things . . . Words you don't mean, but you can't take back. You lash out, because you're hurting so bad, you want someone else to hurt as well. You only want to wound. But you end up killing. (*Pause.*) I miss my daughter. She's three you know.

SUSAN: (*Gently.*) Yes. You told us.

(They pause for a moment, and drink their drinks.)

GEORGE: It's weird isn't it? Why, when there are so many happy things in life, do you remember the pain?

JANICE: Because there is generally someone to attach it to. Someone to hate or someone to despise. Happiness is general. Pain is specific. When I was first here I was bullied. I mean, nothing much. Just a kind of petty, niggling bullying. It's like when it just drizzles with rain. It's not a storm, but you get just as wet. I was so scared and miserable. And you know I can still remember the people who did it. And I still hate them.

GEORGE: Oh come on Jan. I mean, all kids go through that kind of stuff. Name calling, gangs, that sort of thing. Hate is a bit strong, surely?

JANICE: No, no, I don't think it is. I met Sarah Jenkins over there. As I came in. She said hello, but I couldn't speak to her. I couldn't. That girl made my life hell. Even now I want to . . . Well, let's just say she'd better not stray too near the trifle. And the worst thing is, all the things they say about you, you start to believe it. You start to think that maybe you are as bad as they say you are. Even now, I still struggle with that. All I want is someone to love me for me. Not for what I do, not for what I think. Just for who I am. I know that Oak loves me. I think he loves me. But I don't know if he really loves the me inside. But then maybe I don't either.

(There is a pause. Then they realise.)

SUSAN: (*Disbelief.*) You're going out with someone called "Oak"?

JANICE: "Oak Mooncrescent." When he became an environmental campaigner and started protesting, he changed it by deed poll.

GEORGE: That's nice. Maybe one day we'll hear the patter of tiny acorns.

JANICE: (*Annoyed.*) He's a very deep person.

JOHNNY: Of course he is. He's living down a hole.

GEORGE: I don't know. Look at us all. Middle-aged, depressed, dysfunctional. What a fine tribute to the old school we turned out to be.

JANICE: It's not just us. Everyone's like it. Just a mass of guilt and missed opportunities.

SUSAN: (*Quoting.*) "Forgive us our trespasses, as we forgive others . . ." We used to stand here every Monday morning and say that.

JANICE: Yeah. I've always wondered about that. What is a trespass?

JOHNNY: You should know. You're the one living up someone else's tree.

SUSAN: No. It's a sin. It's all the stuff we do to each other that we shouldn't do. People tread all over you. You tread all over them. That's real trespassing.

JOHNNY: Wouldn't it be great if we could go back? You know, wipe the slate clean, start again. No guilt, no pain, no hate. Get rid of it all. That would be great.

GEORGE: *(Looking at his watch.)* It's late. Come on, we'd better be going.

          *(*Johnny *stays sitting. The others get up to go.)*

JANICE: I'd better be moving along as well.

GEORGE: *(To* Janice.*)* We'll give you a lift. *(To* Johnny.*)* Well, it's been great seeing you again.

JOHNNY: Yeah. We must get depressed together more often.

GEORGE: Keep in touch, eh?

JANICE: See you, Johnny.

JOHNNY: Yeah, bye. Give my love to Oak. I hope he doesn't get woodworm.

          *(*George *and* Janice *leave.)*

SUSAN: I'm sure things will sort themselves out. *(She kisses* Johnny *goodbye.)* Look after yourself.

JOHNNY: Yeah. And you.

She exits. Johnny *pulls his wallet from his pocket and takes out the photo of his daughter. He sits, staring at the photo, until the lights fade.*

John the Symbolic Washer of Dirty People
by Stephen Deal

CAST

JASON

JOHN THE BAPTIST

The theme of this sketch is identity. John the Baptist is one of the most unique characters in a Bible packed with interesting people. His uncompromising stance on the need for repentance both drew people to him and frightened people away. He died because he didn't care who heard his message even if it was the last thing they wanted to hear. The key was that John knew who he was and his role in God's plan. This gave him the confidence to take his stand and stick to it.

Jason has all the depth of formica. He mistakes image for identity. To stage this piece I would have John seated with his back to the audience. He remains perfectly still and calm as Jason paces back and forth in front of him. The contrast between the two will serve to underline Jason's vacuity. However you choose to costume John he should appear rugged and solid. (Because his back is to the audience it avoids the need for a beard.) Jason should be dressed as smartly as possible.

John the Baptist *sits on a chair.* Jason, *an image consultant, remains standing.*

JASON: John, John, John what are we to do with you? No, don't say anything, I'm thinking. The muse is upon me. Thank goodness someone saw fit to call me in. We could have had a disaster on our hands.

(Jason refers to some notes he has on a clipboard.)

It says here you are a prophet. What does that entail? No don't tell me it doesn't matter. All that I need to know is that you are a public figure with an image problem. And as a professional image consultant let me tell you image is everything.

Let us start with the name shall we? Hmm . . . John. That's good. Simple, straightforward, honest. The John part's great, we'll keep it. I'm a little more worried about the Baptist bit. John the Baptist. It has a ring to it I'll give you that. John the Baptist. My worry is that not everyone will know what a Baptist is. Perhaps we should consider John the Symbolic Washer of Dirty People? . . . No? Never mind, we'll come back to that.

Moving on. John, I like you. I like you a lot. You're an interesting man. Unique. Now sometimes unique is good and sometimes it's a distraction. Frankly in your case it's not good. It's a matter of consumer brand affiliation. The public can't relate to a man dressed in camel hair. I suggest we put you in a costume that befits your status. I see silk, I see blue, I see purple. I want your clothes to shout "Look at me! I'm important". At the moment they shout "Look at me! I need a boutique".

I think we need to lose the beard. Perhaps we should move to a goatee? What do you think? No, don't say anything, I can tell you love it. I'll organise a stylist.

(Refers to notes.)

Now, let's see . . . It says here you stand in a river up to your waist while you do your thing. Now, John, do we *need* the water? No, no, think about it. You've got good legs and people just can't see them. Also I think this business of you pouring water over people needs a rethink. You may be liable if someone catches a cold. The last thing we need is a law suit. What about if you stood by the side of the river and asked people to think wet thoughts. Wouldn't that work just as well?

(Refers to notes.)

According to these notes you eat locusts and honey. Are you mad? Don't you realise you're going to alienate both the vegetarian and the dentistry lobbies? I'm a great one for a macrobiotic diet but people will think you're weird.

I think we need to work on your speeches. "Repent ye: for the kingdom of heaven is at hand." You must be crazy thinking you are going to get anywhere with a message about repentance. People don't want to hear that they've got to stop doing what they enjoy. It's just not "on message". We've got to put some spin on the whole "Repent ye" thing. It's too harsh. How about "Think twice: the kingdom of heaven is a viable option"?

Think image John. Image, image, image. When your average man in the desert looks at you – do they see someone who makes them feel all warm and fuzzy inside? Do they see someone they'd like to invite into their homes and perhaps share some beaujolais nouveau with? We want people to see the real you, John, but we want them to see the real John we want them to see and not be distracted by the real, real John that we don't want them to see. Do you follow? Of course you do.

The trouble, John, is that you're not very popular with the people who matter. The common man or woman may flock to see and hear you do your thing, but the movers and shakers who shape public opinion just aren't impressed.

If you listen to me, John, I think we can turn public opinion around. I believe we can repackage you. Presentation is the key. Let's forget about the Prophet thing and go for re-branding you as an entertainer. I'll arrange for you to attend some drama lessons. And what about dance? Another client of mine is having his daughter take some lessons.

It's been great chatting to you. I feel like we've really bonded. You just toddle off back to the wilderness and I'll launch our campaign. We'll do lunch some time.

(Jason's mobile phone rings.)

Excuse me John, busy, busy, busy.

(Answers phone.)

Hello? Oh hi! Herod! I was just talking about you. I've met this absolutely wonderful prophet you simply must network with. You'll love him to pieces. I'll introduce you.

(Barely glancing at John.*)* Ciao, John.

Music for the Entertaining Angels Revue

Nigel, Play that Tune: Using the Music

In performing an *Entertaining Angels* revue, we have already suggested that you should include around six pieces of music. Further information on the thinking behind this is given on pages 9–10. However you decide to use the music (whether with a live band or recorded), the following additional information will be of help, particularly regarding the licences you will need to obtain.

Live Performance

Music copying licence

Entertaining Angels contains the music and lyrics for six songs by Michael Card which we have chosen for their lyrical strength and broad musical appeal. This will enable one musician to learn and perform the songs. If you need to copy music, however, you may do this provided you have a copying licence with an extension to copy music from Christian Copyright Licencing. (The standard licence is for words only.) It is a condition of this licence that you print your licence number on any copies reproduced. You can obtain this licence from:

> Christian Copyright Licensing, 26 Gildredge Road, Eastbourne, BN21 4SA;
> Tel. 01323 417 711; Fax 01323 417 722; e-mail: info@ccli.co.uk

Alternatively you could purchase extra copies of this publication or, for 20p per page and a £5 administration fee per order, obtain copying permission from CopyCare Ltd who administer Michael Card's music in the UK:

> CopyCare Ltd, PO Box 77, Hailsham, East Sussex, BN27 3EF;
> Tel. 01323 840 942; Fax 01323 849 942; e-mail: music@copycare.com

Performance licence

Before performing *Entertaining Angels* music you need to check that your venue is licensed for public music performances. While a local arts centre probably will be licensed, the chances are that your church hall won't be unless you have regular music concerts there. In this case you will need to obtain a performance licence. The cost of this will be around £10 to £25, depending on the size of the venue. The only exception for this is where the songs are used strictly within the context of a worship service where no licence is required. For this licence, contact:

> Performing Rights Society, 29–33 Berners Street, London W1P 4AA;
> Tel. 0171 580 5544; Fax 0171 306 4550

Further Michael Card music

If you would like to use further songs by Michael Card, a songbook *The Life Triology* is available from Alliance Music in the UK and further songbooks can be ordered from Michael Card Music in the USA (addresses below).

Using recorded music

Using recorded music for some or all of the songs may save on fingers and music rehearsals, but you will also need a licence for this. Contact:

> Phonographic Performance Limited (PPL), Ganton House, 14–22 Ganton Street, London, W1V 1LB; Tel. 0171 437 0311; Fax 0171 734 2986. A year's licence costs around £30.

Recordings by Michael Card

Five of the six songs included in this book are currently available in recorded form on two CDs/cassettes:

"So Many Books", That's What Faith Must Be" and "Joy in the Journey" are included on *Joy in the Journey*. **CD: SPD** 1435; Cassette: **SPC** 1435.

The songs "The Final Word", "Scandalon" and "Joy in the Journey" appear on *The Life Trilogy*. **CD: SPD** 8511712; Cassette: **SPC** 1171.

Both recordings should be easily obtained from Christian bookshops. In case of difficulty, you can also order them from:

> Alliance Music, Waterside House, Woodley Headland, Milton Keynes, MK6 3BY; Tel. 01908 677074; Fax 01908 677760; website http://www.alliancemusic.co.uk/

A full range of Michael's recordings and songbooks for ordering, together with information about his current output, can be found on Michael Card's website: http://michaelcard.com or from:

> Michael Card Music, PO Box 586, Franklin TN, 37065-0586, USA.

So Many Books...

This song was written in Beijing during a Bible smuggling trip with members of the Bible League.
It is dedicated to all the courageous men and women, the teachers and pastors, who labor for the kingdom in China.

Words and Music by
MICHAEL CARD

1. There __ is a hun - ger, a long - ing for bread, __ And so __ comes the call __ for the poor __ to be fed. __ More hun-
(2. There'll) __ come a time, __ the pro - phets would say, __ When the joy of man-kind __ will be with - ered a - way. __ A want,

towards the Light.

2. There'll_ -pen a Bi - ble and move___ towards the Light,___ O-

-pen a Bi - ble and move___ towards the Light.__ The Word___ won't go out___ ex - cept_

33

_ it re-turn__ Full,__ o - ver - flow - ing. And so___ we must learn.____

So man-y books,__ so lit-tle time.__ So__ man-y hun-ger, so__ man-y blind.

Starv-ing for words,__ they must wait__ in the night__ To o - pen a Bi - ble and move__

towards the Light, ___ O - pen a Bi - ble and move ___ towards the Light, ___ O -

- pen a Bi - ble and move ___ towards the Light. ___

SCANDALON

Words By Michael Card

Music by Michael Card

se - ers and the proph - ets had __ fore-told __ it long a - go, __ that the
(2.)long the path of life __ there lies __ this stub - born scan - dal-on, __ — and

Coda

(Guitar solo)

Voice:

He will be___ the truth___ that will of - fend them one and all; the

99

Could It Be

Words and Music by
MICHAEL CARD

can't hear with our ears._____ They say to live__ by some-thing that you

fool - ish and in - sane,_____ to the ones who care__ to seek__ you, to the

can't see with your eyes._____ Is there real - ly an - y pur-pose to this

ones who nev - er will._____ You are the on - ly an - swer, e - ven

fool - ish ex - er - cise?_____ Could it be You make__ Your pres-ence known__ so

still.__ Could it be You make__ Your pres-ence known__ so

mf

11

mf

mf

mf

of - ten by __ Your ab - sence? Could it be that ques - tions tell us more than

an - swers ev - er do?_____ Could it be that You __ would real - ly rath - er die_____

3rd time to Coda

__ than live with - out __ us? Could it be the on - ly an - swer that means

1. an - y - thing_____ is You?_____

That's What Faith Must Be

Words and Music by
MICHAEL CARD

THE FINAL WORD

Words by Michael Card

Music by Michael Card

In a slow two feel ♩ = 138

1. You and me, we use so very man - y clum - sy words.
(2.) so the Fa - ther's fond - est thought took on flesh and bone.

The noise of what we of - ten say is not
He spoke the liv - ing, lu - mi - nous Word, at once

so was born___ the ba - by who would die___ to make___ it ___ mine!___

2. And ___

JOY IN THE JOURNEY

Words By Michael Card

Music by Michael Card

won - der and wild - ness to_ life, and free - dom for_
ter - ni - ty, strand - ed in_ time, and wea - ry of_

3rd time to Coda

those who_ o - bey. And all those who seek_ it shall
strug - gling_ with sin. For - get not the hope_ that's be -

find_ it, a par - don for_ all who_ be - lieve._
fore_ you, and nev - er stop_ count - ing_ the cost._

Hope for the hope - less and sight for the
Re - mem - ber the hope - less - ness when you were

Other resources from Bible Society

Ten-minute Miracle Plays

Margaret Cooling

The miracle plays which educated and entertained people in the Middle Ages are adapted to bring the Bible to life in schools and churches today. This book contains all you need to use the plays in a variety of settings – from a simple reading to a fully staged performance. Back-up material, for church or classroom use, is also included to show how the Bible stories can have relevance to life today. *Ten-minute Miracle Plays* offers an active approach to the Bible in which everyone can enjoy playing a part.

- Includes poetry and music
- Plays may be photocopied

Price £15.99 (ISBN 0564 087750)

Reel Issues

by Ian Maher

The average UK resident buys one video and rents four more every year, while 72% of young adults (15- to 34-year-olds) are regular cinema-goers. The potential influence of films, especially among age-groups least represented in the churches, is enormous. In this practical guidebook, Ian Maher shows how popular films can be used to reach out to people for whom the Bible is currently a closed book.

Features:

- How film-watching can connect us with modern people's views of the world, and how to find biblical answers to their concerns
- How to plan and structure a film-watching and discussion
- Ten current films examined with detailed guidelines on how to use them in exploring the five Open Book themes of Identity, Freedom, Justice, Hope and Forgiveness.

Price £4.50 (ISBN 0564 041262)

Splashes of God-light

Catherine Bowness, Terence Copley, Sarah Lane, Heather Savini, editors

Contains over twenty biblical stories retold for today in ways that will stir the imagination and give fresh insights into biblical episodes.

Writers include well-known Christian and Jewish contributors like Frank Topping, Fay Sampson, Trevor Dennis, Frances Young and Dan Cohn-Sherbok. Each contributor also explains the significance the story has for them. The stories can be used both for performance or personal reading.

Price £5.99 (ISBN 0564 040568)

Publications available from Christian bookshops or, in case of difficulty, direct from:

Bible Society, Stonehill Green, Westlea, Swindon SN5 7DG

Tel: 01793 418100; Fax: 01793 418118;

E-mail: info@bfbs.org.uk

Website: www.biblesociety.org.uk